The NAMES OF JESUS

by
Anton Sorg, O. Carm.

translated by
Matthew J. O'Connell

THE LITURGICAL PRESS
Collegeville   Minnesota

Cover design Christ the King. *Maria Laach.*

THE NAMES OF JESUS is the authorized English translation of *Namen, die Sein Wesen Nennen*, copyright Anton Sorg, O.Carm.

Nihil obstat: William G. Heidt, O.S.B., *Censor deputatus. Imprimatur:* ✝ George H. Speltz, D.D., Bishop of St. Cloud. June 15, 1976.

ISBN 0-8146-0920-1

CONTENTS

PREFACE

St. Joan of Arc, the Maid of Orléans, was executed in the public square of Rouen. The pyre had been lit and the flames were already licking at her when she cried out, so loudly that the whole city could hear her, "Jesus! Jesus! Jesus!" The name of Jesus gave her hope as she was dying.

The angel Gabriel had told Mary of the name "Jesus," the name by which men would address the Savior. It means "salvation, redemption." Jesus had other names as well, but they are all clarifications of the mystery hidden in the name Jesus.

"To preach his name" meant, for the writers of Sacred Scripture, "to make known his true nature." So, too, when Jesus gave himself other names or titles, his intention was to make his true nature known to us.

The German astronomer Johann Kepler spent his life studying the courses of the stars. The Jesuit Erich Wasmann spent his life studying the ways of the ants. How much more beautiful and blessed a thing it is for us to search out the mystery of Jesus and his mother! But we must remember that Jesus reveals the secrets contained in his name only to those who love him.

I hope that the following chapters, unworthy though they are of the great mystery they treat, will help the reader in some little way to a deeper knowledge and love of Jesus.

The Author

PRAYER

Jesus Christ, eternal Word, divine Master, you are the Father's glory and the reflection of his being. You told us: "He who loves me will be loved by my Father. I too will love him and reveal myself to him" (John 14:21). Grant that we may love you so deeply and fervently that we may be worthy to be more fully enlightened concerning your divine being! For it is there that we shall, according to your own words, find the secret of eternal life: We shall learn that our heavenly Father is the only true God and that you are his Son, Jesus Christ, who came to earth to be our teacher, brother, friend, spouse, and high priest of our salvation. Enlighten our souls with a ray of the divine light that shone resplendent on Mount Tabor so that our faith in your divinity may be strengthened, our hope in your merits increased, and our love for your adorable Person be ever more ardent and deep.

Yes, Father, I believe! I will repeat what you have told me: The same Jesus who dwells within me through faith and Holy Communion is your Son! Because you said it, I believe it, and because I believe it, I worship your Son and do homage to him. Through him and with him may all honor and glory be given to you, heavenly Father, and to the Holy Spirit, forever and ever.

THE SON OF MARY

The people of Nazareth were sure they knew Jesus. To them he was simply the son of Mary. "They said . . . 'Is this not the carpenter, the son of Mary?'" (Mark 6:3). They meant the words in a derogatory sense, because by referring thus to his antecedents, they wanted to make things too difficult in his native town and thus get rid of him and his blasphemous claims. To the evangelists, to the Church, and to us, Jesus is the Son of Mary in an entirely different sense than he was for his fellow-townsmen and for his adversaries, the Pharisees.

The name "son of Mary" expresses for us the mystery of the Incarnation and of our redemption. That is why we speak the words with deepest reverence and heartfelt gratitude. Jesus is not the son of an earthly father but the Son of the heavenly Father from all eternity. He would simply withdraw from us if we were to refuse to see in him the Son of God, but we would also lose him if we were unwilling to see in him the son of Mary.

As son of Mary, Jesus owes her his human nature. He could have entered human life by taking a human nature created directly out of nothing, but he chose to be born of a woman and did not shrink from entering Mary's womb. How amazing that the divine Word should make his incarnation depend on the free consent of a woman! For thousands of years mankind had been yearning for a redeemer, yet when God decided to begin the climactic stage of redemption, he sent the angel Gabriel to Mary to ask for her consent. The choirs of angels and God himself waited silently for Mary's agreement. Mary answered: "I am the servant of the Lord. Let it be done to me as you say" (Luke 1:38), and at that moment the second Person of the Blessed Trinity became a man in Mary's womb. It was from her pure blood and her womb that the God-man came into existence, being born of Mary the Virgin and having received from her his nature and powers. Consequently, there was an ineffably close bond between Mary and Jesus: She was his mother and he was her son. That bond will never be broken.

The angels told the shepherds that they would find the child and his mother in the stable at Bethlehem (Luke 2:8-16). Later on, Jesus would have himself presented in the Temple by his mother, thus beginning the sacrifice that would be completed on Calvary. Mary nourished and tended to the child.

The wise men from the East "found the child with Mary his mother. They prostrated themselves and did him homage" (Matthew 2:11). Then, safe in his mother's arms, the divine child took refuge in Egypt (Matthew 2:13).

During his hidden life in Nazareth, Jesus was under the protection and influence of his mother, and, as son of Mary, he felt himself to be a happy man. With her he prayed, went to the synagogue, and spoke of the mysteries of God's kingdom which he himself would later preach to men. Love established a deep harmony between these two souls.

At the beginning of his public life, Jesus manifested himself for the first time in a miracle that was performed at his mother's request. After that, the evangelists tell us repeatedly, Mary accompanied Jesus and his apostles on their apostolic journeys.

The supreme work of Jesus, and the central mystery of all his mysteries, was his bitter Passion and death. In the carrying out of this work, Jesus wished to be associated in a very special way with his mother. He wanted to offer through her, as it were, the sacrifice of the Cross, which would bring us men the forgiveness of sins and the divine life of grace. The depth and intimacy of Jesus' relationship to his mother is revealed to us in his words from the Cross: "Woman, there is your son" and "There is your mother" (John 19:26-27). These simple words, spoken as Jesus was dying on the Cross for the salvation of the world, show us how tender his love for his mother was and how the two of them shared everything.

Everything a child owes its mother — temperament, nurture, protection, loving intimacy — Jesus owed Mary, and in a very perfect way. And he thanked her by his love for her. Never has any son loved his mother so deeply and intensely as Jesus loved his holy mother. He said on one occasion that his love for men was so great as to make him die for them: "There is no greater love than this: to lay down one's life for one's friends" (John 15:13). But who was more closely linked to Jesus by the bonds of friendship than Mary? It was for her, first and foremost, that Jesus was willing to die, for thus he would pay the price for her privileges. We are justified in saying that among all the children of men Mary was the primary object of Christ's love in his Passion.

Jesus loved his mother and made known to her the depths of the mysteries concealed in his life; from her he had no secrets, and everything the Father communicated to him, he communicated to her. Mary in turn had a deep understanding — so far as a human heart can — of the revelations brought by her Son, and she accepted them eagerly.

Jesus loved his mother. Even as he hung on the Cross he provided for her by entrusting her to the disciple whom he loved. Then, showing his love for her to the utmost, he took her, body and soul, into heaven. And because on earth she had played so intimate a part in all the mysteries of redemption, he crowned her in heaven with power as well as glory. He set his dear mother at his right hand so that she might dispose of the supernatural treasures of eternal life, thus exercising a right which her unique dignity as God's mother bestowed on her.

Because Jesus loved his mother more than any other creature, he was obedient to her. The evangelists tell us that Jesus was obedient to Mary and Joseph (Luke 2:51). To a certain extent Mary shared in the eternal Father's authority over the holy humanity of his Son, and Jesus obeyed his mother until he was thirty years old. Mary then continued her maternal work until the day "when the ripe fruit dropped quite naturally from the branch" (Garonne). It was precisely because Jesus was so perfectly obedient to his mother that she was so taken by surprise when the twelve-year-old boy manifested his independence as God's Son and asserted that he must be about his Father's business. Jesus could say with regard to his dear mother no less than to his heavenly Father: "I always do what pleases him" (John 8:29).

* * *

As Christians, we must try to be like Christ, even to be images of him. That means that since Jesus was Son both of God and of Mary, we too must be children both of God and of Mary.

We become children of God through Jesus, who became our brother and has bestowed on us his Spirit, the Spirit of sonship, by whose power we say: *Abba*! Dear Father! (cf. Rom. 8:15). We become children of Mary by the will of Jesus. We do not become her children in a bodily sense, of course, for only Jesus possesses that privilege, but neither do we become her children in a purely figurative sense. We do not call Mary our mother simply because she loves us (as a sick person might call a nurse "mother" because he experiences her loving care). No, she is truly our mother, but in a spiritual way.

The all-wise Lord, who knows man's deep need of a mother, has given her to us. The human person calls out for a mother. "Mother" is the first word many children say, and often one of the last words a person says before death. The human being yearns for a mother in times of anxiety and distress, and wants to share his joys with a mother. For this reason the day of a mother's death is one of the darkest days in a person's life.

God did not intend that this inborn desire of the heart for a mother should go unfulfilled. Now, is the human person not to have a mother to whom he may go in the anxieties, cares, and joys of the supernatural life? Yes, God, who himself loves us with a mother's love (Is. 66:13), wants us to have a mother in our supernatural life as well as in our natural life. The order of redemption, after all, parallels the order of creation. As God set Eve, the mother of all the living, alongside Adam, so he has set Mary, the mother of supernatural life, alongside Jesus, the new Adam. She is to communicate, nourish, and protect, as a loving mother, the life Christ merited for us.

Mary, our mother, is an incomparably wonderful mystery, a loving heritage from the Lord. The gift comes from the same loving heart that gave us the Bread of life.

*   *   *

Mary, our mother, conceived us as her spiritual children. When the angel told her that she had found favor with

God and had been chosen to become mother of the Redeemer, Mary gave her consent to God's whole plan of
redemption: "I am the servant of the Lord. Let it be done
to me as you say" (Luke 1:38). With these words she gave
the God-man his human existence.

In his encyclical *Ad diem illum*, issued February 2,
1904, in honor of the fiftieth anniversary of the definition of
the Immaculate Conception, Pope Pius X wrote:

> When Mary carried the Savior in her womb, she may
> be said also to have carried all those whose lives the
> Savior's life contained within itself. Therefore, all of
> us who are united to Christ and who, in the Apostle's
> words, "are members of his body" (Eph. 5:30), have
> come forth from Mary's womb like a body united to
> its head. Consequently, in a spiritual and mystical
> way we are the children of Mary and she is mother
> of us all, a mother in the spirit indeed, yet truly
> the mother of Christ's members which we are (cf.
> St. Augustine, *On Virginity*, ch. 6).

According to the same encyclical, Christ made Mary
an effective agent in the work of redemption. At the moment
when Mary conceived Jesus in the flesh, she conceived us
in the spirit; being mother of the Head, she became mother
of the members as well; being mother of the Redeemer, she
became mother of the redeemed; being mother of the Son
of God, she became mother of the children of God.

St. Gertrude the Great tells us that

> One day, at the liturgy, as the words "first-born
> child of the Virgin Mother of God" were being read,
> she reflected that the Lord might better be called
> "only child," since the immaculate Virgin Mary bore
> only Jesus whom she had conceived by the Holy
> Spirit. But the Blessed Virgin herself answered her
> in a charming, friendly way: "No, my Jesus is more

fittingly called "first born" than "only child" because I bore him first, and after him — or better through him — I bore all his brothers as my children, and I love them all with a mother's heart" (*Herald of Divine Love*, IV, 3).

After Mary had conceived us as her children, she brought us forth to supernatural life in the blessed hour when her Son died on the Cross for us. In his encyclical on the Mystical Body (June 29, 1943), Pope Pius XII calls Mary the holy mother of all the members of Christ. Then he says:

> It was she, the second Eve, who, free from all sin, original or personal, and always most intimately united with her Son, offered Him on Golgotha to the Eternal Father for all the children of Adam, sin-stained by his unhappy fall, and her mother's rights and mother's love were included in the holocaust. Thus she who, according to the flesh was the mother of our Head, through the added title of pain and glory became, according to the Spirit, the mother of all his members.

As Mary stood by the Cross, she was directly co-operating with her Son in his sacrificial offering of himself, for the Savior's suffering was shared by his mother as by no other human being. After Jesus, Mary was the one who most fully entered into the sacrificial suffering by which our redemption was effected. In those hours she endured birth pangs for all of us, and we are the children of her pain.

It is not without significance that during the very time when Mary was suffering the pains of our birth to supernatural life, Jesus, by his third word on the Cross, gave her her new maternal role. Against this background his words take on a deeper meaning. "Seeing his mother there with the disciple whom he loved, Jesus said to his mother, 'Woman, there is your son.' In turn he said to the disciple, 'There is your mother'" (John 19:26-27). John here represented all of us; it was to all of us that Jesus was giving his mother.

St. Paul speaks of Jesus as the "first-born of many brothers" (Rom. 8:29). But if Jesus is our first-born brother, then we are called to be like him. If Jesus wanted to become our brother by taking a human nature from Mary and becoming one of our race, is it any wonder that at his death he should give us as mother of grace her who was his own bodily mother? The word of Jesus, as the word of the eternal Son of God, is almighty and full of divine power. Therefore it roused in the heart of the Blessed Virgin a maternal, tender love for all who by grace had become or would become the brothers of Jesus. Who can doubt that the Virgin Mother accepted the last wish of her Son with the same silent, loving, humble, self-sacrificing yes that once she spoke at Nazareth? Jesus' words should fill us with the same love for Mary with which they filled John's soul, for of him Scripture says: "From that hour onward, the disciple took her into his care" (John 19:27).

Mary probably came to understand fully her vocation to spiritual motherhood when the Holy Spirit descended upon her at Pentecost. From that day forward, Mary carried out her maternal task by the power of the Holy Spirit, and she will continue to carry it out until the end of time. Pope Pius XII wrote in his encyclical on the Mystical Body: "She continues to have for the Mystical Body of Christ, born of the pierced Heart of the Savior, the same motherly care and ardent love with which she cherished and fed the Infant Jesus in the crib."

Formerly all her loving concern had been lavished

on the historical Jesus; now it is lavished on the mystical Christ. Her only wish is to make all of us authentic, courageous Christians and effective members of the Mystical Body of Jesus Christ, and to "form that perfect man who is Christ come to full stature" (Eph. 4:13).

No mother ever loses her love and concern for the children she bore in pain. Mary never ceases her care for the souls she brought to birth in pain as she stood beside the Cross. She leads these souls along the paths of holiness. St. Bonaventure writes: "I have never read of a saint who did not have a special devotion to the glorious Virgin."

This heavenly mother communicates to the soul a living and life-giving knowledge of Jesus Christ. She knew Jesus as no other human being knew him; she shared truly and deeply in the life of her Son. She is able, therefore, to lead souls to this kind of living knowledge of Jesus and to help them etch the portrait of Jesus with a loving hand within themselves and in their lives.

Mary gains for many of these souls a vocation to the priesthood or religious life and helps them, once they answer the call, to live up to it fully. She keeps the spirit of faith alive in families that honor her. She spreads her mantle to protect the children of God against the loss of the life of grace. Since she herself became our mother in pain, she has a special place in her maternal heart for those who suffer in body or mind. Numerous places of pilgrimage, shrines, hymns, and prayers bear witness to the trust Christians have in the maternal love of Mary for them, as does the confidence that finds expression in their petitions for a favorable hearing. Only loving souls really comprehend that Mary is the spiritual mother of God's children.

In his farewell discourse at the Last Supper, Jesus said: "He who loves me will be loved by my Father. I too will love him and reveal myself to him" (John 14:21).

So too, it is only those who love who understand the mystery of Mary, our mother. Happy the man who understands it!

Pope John XXIII understood it. We are told that one of his favorite ejaculatory prayers all his life was: "Mary, my mother, in you I trust." On his deathbed he repeated this prayer over and over, and when he could no longer speak, others said it for him. Each time, he would make the words his own with a little nod. It was to the words, "Mary, my mother, in you I trust," that he died.

We shall never be able to count and weigh the proofs of love our earthly mothers have given us. Much less will we be able to count and weigh those given us by our spiritual mother, Mary.

* * *

We should love Mary as our mother. It is true that in our love we cannot bestow gifts on her such as her Son bestowed, but she does not expect that of us. We can, however, show our love for her in other ways. We can do it, for example, by praising her for her privileges and rejoicing over the incomparable advantages Jesus gave her. By so doing, we shall acquire something of Jesus' attitude toward her who was his mother. Furthermore, we can, especially through the *Magnificat,* thank God for all the graces he gave Mary, just as if they were our own.

A very good way to show our love for our heavenly mother is to invoke her with confidence. A mother appreciates her children's confidence in her more than any other gifts they may give her. Nothing gives a mother greater joy than to have her children come to her trustingly. Our heavenly mother experiences that same joy when we confidently invoke her as Mother of Grace, Refuge of Sinners, Help of Christians, and Consoler of the Afflicted.

Mary is happy to make our needs known to him who gave her to us as our mother. And the Lord in turn is happy to receive the petitions of his mother and ours. If Jesus cured the Canaanite woman's daughter when she asked him, will he not be ready to intervene and help at the request of his mother and ours? Mary did not receive the power of the keys from the Savior as St. Peter did, but she does have the key to the Sacred Heart of Jesus.

The high altar by Michael Pacher in the Church of St. Wolfgang (Upper Austria) shows the crowning of Mary. Christ the Lord has the globe in his hands, and the hands of Mary are helping to support it. The viewer may look at the picture from any angle he wishes, but he will always see Mary gazing at the world with love; she is using her position in order to intercede.

Mary's intercession for her children does not mean that they are spared all suffering or are relieved of it. The Lord did not exempt Mary herself from suffering. In fact, she became the Queen of Martyrs and the Sorrowful Mother. But it is precisely this that enables her to console us, for we know that in all our troubles she, the Sorrowful Mother, is close to us. It was a great source of strength for Jesus on the Cross to know that Mary was there. So it will be a source of strength for us to know that the Sorrowful Mother with her loving heart is at our side.

We show our love for Mary in a very special way by trying to become like Jesus so that he may live in us. He wants to live in us as both Son of the Father and Son of Mary. He wants to dwell in our hearts through faith, which enables us to live in and with Jesus, to create a likeness to him within us, and to act in accordance with his example.

Mary's greatest joy is to see rich graces flowing into

us from the holy humanity of her Son, in whom the fullness of grace dwells. These graces make us like the Father's beloved Son. The Gospels have preserved for us only a few statements by Mary. The last words we hear from her lips are those she spoke to the servants at the marriage feast of Cana: "Do whatever he tells you" (John 2:5). Her words echo those of the eternal Father: "This is my beloved Son on whom my favor rests. Listen to him" (Matthew 17:5). We should apply these words of Mary to ourselves: "Whatever my Son tells you to do, do it!" That is the best possible way of honoring our heavenly mother, for her dearest wish is to see her divine Son loved, glorified, and exalted.

Jesus, Son of the eternal Father and Son of the Virgin Mary, live in my soul through the power of your Holy Spirit and in the fullness of your might. Let me share in your mystery and help me to live in childlike love of God our Father and of our dear mother Mary.

Mother of the Incarnate Word, your Son said: "As often as you did it for one of my least brothers, you did it for me" (Matthew 25:40). I am the least of your Son's servants. In his name I come before you to ask your help. Mary, show you are a mother! Mother of Jesus and our mother, by your power over him and your mercy toward us, may Jesus receive our prayers from your hands! To give us life, he willed to be born of you and be your Son.

THE TEACHER

What is truth? Who will show us the way to wisdom? These are man's age-old questions. Throughout history men have every now and then come forward thinking they had the answers: a Buddha or a Confucius, a Plato or an Aristotle, a Cicero or a Seneca, to name but a few of earlier times. Their desire was to be teachers of the truth and to show men the path of wisdom. But as the sun surpasses the stars in brightness, so does Jesus surpass in wisdom all the other teachers mankind has had. He had every right to call himself the only true teacher: "Avoid being called teachers. Only one is your teacher, the Messiah" (Matthew 23:10). Later on, he would say to Pilate: "The reason I was born, the reason why I came into the world, is to testify to the truth" (John 18:37).

In the church of Hagia Sophia at Istanbul, there is a mosaic depicting Christ as a teacher. Jesus Christ is the teacher of a holy wisdom; indeed, he is himself holy Wisdom, and it is eternal. Therefore he could say of himself: "The heavens and the earth will pass away but my words will not pass" (Matthew 24:35).

Many people sought out Jesus the teacher. Individuals came to him by themselves. How attentively the Samaritan woman at Jacob's well or Nicodemus in the night or Mary in Bethany listened to his words! But the crowds also came after him. One such crowd stayed with him for three days in the desert, oblivious to hunger, thirst, and weariness, for men wanted to hear his words and found no sacrifice too great. These crowds were amazed at Jesus' words, for they felt that he spoke quite differently from the scribes. When Jesus had dismissed the crowds after a discourse, he would continue to address his disciples, initiating them more fully into the mysteries of which he had been speaking.

His first and best audience was his mother, Mary. Before he began to preach publicly to the crowds, he had already been sharing his wisdom with her. She listened to him with even greater attention than the other Mary at Bethany did. She reflected on all he said, and there could have been no better field for the seed of his word, since she brought forth more than the hundredfold of fruit. If we realize that Mary was the first to hear the words we now read in the Gospels and that she listened to them with great love, those words will become especially beautiful and precious to us. Moreover, many things Jesus said have come down to us through Mary.

Jesus knew himself to be the teacher foretold by the prophet, as he showed when he applied the words of Isaias to himself: "The spirit of the Lord is upon me; therefore he has anointed me. He has sent me to bring glad tidings to the poor, to proclaim liberty to captives, recovery of sight to the blind and release to prisoners, to announce a year of favor from the Lord" (Luke 4:18-19; cf. Is. 61:1-2). The prophet was here describing in advance the preaching activity of Jesus. How splendidly Jesus fulfilled the prophecy! He did preach the glad tidings to the poor. He sowed the seed of his word on the mountain, on the lakeshore, in homes, in the boat, in the fields, at banquets, at men's graves, in the Supper room, before the tribunal, and on the Cross. Jesus knew that his doctrine was a necessity for men, and so he was zealous in teaching and preaching. He wanted to work while the light lasted for him.

If Jesus had had twenty or thirty years in which to teach, instead of two or three, what treasures of wisdom he could have given to mankind! Yet even what he gave in a few years is so rich that mankind will never exhaust it. And though there is much more Jesus could have said, he nonetheless said everything, because in him revelation came to its perfect expression.

Even the manner in which Jesus taught was incomparably beautiful. He taught with *complete originality*. Plato sat at the foot of Socrates, Paul at the feet of Gamaliel, Thomas Aquinas at the feet of Albert the Great. But no one could boast that he was in any true sense Jesus' teacher. Jesus had to question no one for information, for he was himself the provident head of the household who brings forth both new and old from his storeroom (cf. Matthew 13:52). He lived in the thought-world of the Old Testament, yet he read the Old Testament, not as a believing student, but as its lord and master. He set his own word over against the word of God, for the highest and final word he carried within his own soul. The truth was for him something immediately evident, something he experienced personally. What he taught was truth out of his own person. That is why he was able to say even the deepest things in a simple way.

Jesus taught with *power*: "He taught with authority and not like their scribes" (Matthew 7:29). His words carried an overwhelming impact, but it was the impact, not of storm and earthquake, but of the gently whispering May breeze. In simple images and parables drawn from the everyday life of the people, he gave concrete form to the mysteries of God's reign. He took the things and persons and events of daily life and turned them into unforgettable symbols of God's eternal thoughts. He used the lilies of the field and the birds of the air to bring home the providence of God; the good shepherd to show God's love; the watchful servant and the workers in the vineyard to show us men how we are to serve God; the children to teach us how we should trust in God and put ourselves at his disposal.

The parables of Jesus are so clear that even a child can

grasp their meaning. Once when I was telling some small children about Jesus the teacher, emphasizing the fact that men in his own day were so glad to listen to him while the men of today quickly tire of hearing God's word, one little fellow said to me: "If Jesus would teach us, we'd be glad to listen, no matter how long."

Yet the parables of Jesus are also so deep that the sharpest minds cannot exhaust them. They have such power that they can rouse any man of good will to want and do what is right. Their power is like that of the little mustard seed that breaks through the clods of earth, like that of yeast, which, when put in a closed jar, can crack it. When Jesus said, for example, "Come after me and I will make you fishers of men" (Matthew 4:19), his words caused Peter and his brother immediately to leave their nets and follow him.

Jesus taught with *wisdom*. He was able with incomparable skill to lead his hearers from the visible to the invisible, from the natural to the supernatural. We need only recall his conversation with the Samaritan woman at Jacob's well. To her he was just an ordinary man. Then she recognized that he was a Jew (John 4:9). As the conversation proceeded, she came to perceive more: "I can see you are a prophet" (John 4:19). Then when the woman came to speak of the expected Messiah, Jesus revealed to her what he had thus far revealed to no one else: "I who speak to you am he" (John 4:26). When, finally, Jesus entered the city, many believed in him because of the woman's testimony; but when they themselves had heard him speak, they believed that "this really is the Savior of the world" (John 4:42).

Jesus taught with *gentleness* and *humility*. His words were powerful, yet they were also simple and stirring. He allowed no one to be crushed by his words. He did not break the bruised reed nor extinguish the smoldering flax, but always encouraged, consoled, and awakened to new resolution. How encouraging his words to the adulteress were: "Has no one condemned you? . . . Nor do I condemn you. You may go. But from now on, avoid this sin" (John 8:10-11). Or his words to the sinful woman: "Her many sins are forgiven — because of her great love" (Luke 7:47). Or to Martha at Bethany: "Martha, Martha, you are anxious and upset about many things; one thing only is required. Mary has chosen the better portion and she shall not be deprived of it" (Luke 10:41-42).

Jesus taught *truthfully*. One day the Pharisees "sent their disciples to him, accompanied by the Herodian sympathizers, who said: 'Teacher, we know you are a truthful man and teach God's way sincerely. You court no one's favor and do not act out of human respect . . .'" (Matthew 22:16). Thus even his enemies had to admit his truthfulness. Jesus preached the whole truth, unmixed with any falsehood. He set no traps, but neither did he change his teaching in any way, as merely human teachers do in order to attract hearers.

Jesus knew that the truth is eternal and that only the truth can set men free. That was the truth he wanted to teach men; to it he intended to bear witness, even if it brought disadvantage, persecution, and finally death. St. Paul writes that we should "profess the truth in love" (Eph. 4:15). Well, Jesus preached the truth with love. He might come out sharply against the falsehoods of the Pharisees, yet his words were never wounding. He spoke with kindness to the sick and to sinners. No cheap witticisms, no mockery. Jesus never had to ask anyone's pardon; he never made anyone feel embarrassed. Everything he said was natural, simple, intelligible. Nothing was said obscurely, and Jesus never had to correct, add to, tone down, or take back what he had said. His words were as perfect (more than human) at the beginning of his ministry as they would be at the end of his life. By his own life he made his teaching intelligible and clear, for what he taught was in the last analysis himself, that is, love. His voice was so clear and pure that all else lost its attraction. Anyone who listened to him with an unprejudiced mind was forced to say: "He is a good man" (John 7:12).

We love Jesus the teacher not simply because of his noble manner but also because of his message. He brought a new message to men, a message no one else can make more perfect or complete. But that message requires a wholly new way of thinking and living.

Jesus revealed to men that God and his reign alone give real meaning to human effort. As today, so in Jesus' time, man himself was the focus of human thought and effort. Even the piety of the day turned man's relation to God into a business deal. It was thought that God would have to meet every good work of man with a corresponding reward. Jesus taught that, on the contrary, God is the center and that man must be concerned with God, not vice versa (just as Copernicus would teach men that the sun, not the earth, is the center of the universe, and that the earth moves around the sun, not vice versa). All that men need they must ask of God; only with empty hands can they approach him.

Man must serve God with an undivided heart. He must give God what belongs to him (cf. Matthew 22:21), and adore and serve him alone (Matthew 4:10). Man must love God: "You shall love the Lord your God with your whole heart, with your whole soul, and with all your mind" (Matthew 22:37). "No man can serve two masters. He will either hate one and love the other or be attentive to one and despise the other. You cannot give yourself to God and money" (Matthew 6:24).

God is the supreme goal for man. He wants to give men a share in his life and joy; he invites them to his table and wishes to receive them into his kingdom. In the parable of the royal marriage feast, for example, we see God inviting man to his table. Neither possessions nor earthly joys must be allowed to keep them from accepting the invitation and coming to the feast. The feast is, of course, a symbol of God's kingdom, and those who attend the feast are those who enter that kingdom.

In the parable of the treasure hidden in a field, Jesus was teaching that men must give up everything and bend their efforts to finding and securing the treasure. Through the work and person of Jesus, God's reign over men began and, with it, his glory among men. Men must allow God to rule in them by keeping their hearts open, through faith and repentance, to the message of Jesus. "Seek out . . . his kingship over you, and the rest will follow in turn" (Luke 12:31).

Jesus brought men a new message concerning the Father. He spoke frequently of that Father who is both his Father and ours. He knew the Father as no one else did or could; he lived for him and wished to teach men how they could come to the Father. He himself knew the way, because he had come from the Father. In the most beautiful of all the parables, that of the merciful father, Jesus told of a straying son who came back home to his father. From far off the father saw him coming and was filled with compassion. He ran out to meet him, threw his arms around him, and kissed him. But the son said only: "Father, I have sinned against God and against you; I no longer deserve to be called your son" (Luke 15: 21). The father, however, said to his servants: "'Quick! bring out the finest robe and put it on him; put a ring on his finger and shoes on his feet. Take the fatted calf and kill it. Let us eat and celebrate because this son of mine was dead and has come back to life. He was lost and is found.' Then the celebration began" (Luke 15:22-24).

The brother of the lost son was angry at the celebration and reproached his father for never having given him, the elder son, a kid goat to celebrate with his friends. But the father said to him: "My son, you are with me always, and everything I have is yours" (Luke 15:31). How kind the father is, even to this ungrateful son! The father refused to return the son's bitterness with bitterness.

If an earthly father can be so good, how good must the heavenly Father be! God is not primarily a lawgiver and judge, but a father. Even when he punishes, the punishment is not for its own sake but is a means which God, in his fatherly love, makes use of to save. This Father rejects none of his children, as long as some tiny spark of love is left in them.

God is our Father: such is Jesus' message, his good news, to sinners, to the lonely and the discouraged, to the man at prayer. But if God is our Father, then we must approach him with childlike love and trust. The Lord warns us: "Unless you change and become like little children, you will not enter the kingdom of God" (Matthew 18:3). To the discouraged he says: "Your heavenly Father knows all that you need" (Matthew 6:32). To those who wish to pray: "This is how you are to pray: 'Our Father in heaven . . . '" (Matthew 6:9). God's love for us is the love of a father.

New also was Jesus' message of the infinite value of the human soul. In the parable of the lost sheep, the Lord describes the grief of the shepherd at losing one sheep, his eagerness in searching for it, and his joy at finding it. Even a single sheep means a lot to a shepherd. But of far greater, even infinite, value in God's eyes is a single human soul. It was for the souls of men that God's Son became a man and died on the Cross. All earthly goods taken together do not outweigh in value a single soul which the Lord has redeemed with his own blood. For this reason he can say: "What profit would a man show if he were to gain the whole world and destroy himself [lose his soul] in the process?" (Matthew 16:26). In the eyes of Jesus, the rich farmer who, in his eagerness for earthly riches, forgot to take care of his own soul was a fool. So were the virgins whose lamps were not lit when the bridegroom came, that is, who did not take care of the most important thing — keeping the light of grace in their souls. Even if something be so close and dear to us as eye or foot or hand, we must surrender it if it endangers the soul: "Better to enter life with one eye than be thrown with both into fiery Gehenna" (Matthew 18:9).

To safeguard our soul, we must die to sin and hate anything evil in us. "The man who loves his life loses it, while the man who hates his life in this world preserves it to life eternal" (John 12:25).

Jesus preached a new commandment, a commandment peculiarly his own: that of love for neighbor and enemy. In the parable of the Good Samaritan, Jesus tells us how priest and Levite passed by the man who had been set upon by robbers. "But a Samaritan who was journeying along came on him and was moved to pity at the sight. He approached him and dressed his wounds, pouring in oil and wine. He then hoisted him on his own beast and brought him to an inn, where he cared for him. The next day he took out two silver pieces and gave them to the innkeeper with the request: 'Look after him, and if there is any further expense I will repay you on my way back.'" Jesus ended the discussion by saying, "Then go and do the same" (Luke 10:33-37).

Jesus wants us to love our neighbor; in fact, he makes love of neighbor his commandment to us, a commandment given in the most solemn hour of his life, on the last evening before his death. It was his last will and testament to us, and as such it ought to be especially holy in our eyes. He calls it his "new commandment" (John 13:34).

What was new is the close connection he establishes between this command and the love of God: "The second is like it: 'You shall love your neighbor as yourself'" (Matthew 22:39). He is saying that love for neighbor

flows from love for God. A man is to love his fellows because they are made in God's image and bear the marks
of his hand upon them. Consequently, we are to love men
in God and God in men.

New also was the model given us of such love for
neighbor. Jesus said: "Love one another as I have loved
you. There is no greater love than this: to lay down one's
life for one's friends" (John 15:12-13). Jesus loved us
to the utmost — to a death on a cross. His own, therefore,
should be ready to love each other to the point of giving
their lives for one another.

New, finally, was the scope Jesus gave to the commandment of love of neighbor. The Christian's love is not
to be limited to friends, benefactors, like-minded people, or
fellow-believers. It is to be as all-embracing as God's love,
which makes the warm sun shine even on sinners. It is to
be as comprehensive as the love of Christ, who prayed
for his enemies as he hung on the Cross. Neither the un-
pleasant ways nor the unacceptable views nor even the sins
of others can allow us to turn them away. Thus, in the
parable of the unmerciful servant Jesus requires that we love
even our enemies.

In this parable the king had written off a debt of ten
thousand talents for one of his officials. But then the latter
seized one of his fellow-servants who owed him a hundred
pennies and couldn't pay; he throttled the man and had
him thrown into prison. The king heard of this, summoned
the official, and said to him: "'You worthless wretch! I
cancelled your entire debt when you pleaded with me.
Should you not have dealt mercifully with your fellow
servant, as I dealt with you?' Then in anger the master
handed him over to the torturers until he paid back all
that he owed. My heavenly Father will treat you in exactly the same way unless each of you forgives his brother
from his heart" (Matthew 18:32-25).

Jesus requires that we forgive our fellow-men and

love even our enemies. "Love your enemies, pray for your persecutors. This will prove that you are sons of your heavenly Father, for his sun rises on the bad and the good, he rains on the just and the unjust" (Matthew 5:44-45). We are to love our enemies as brothers. That kind of love is not suggested to us by flesh and blood: it is a reflection in us of God's eternal love. Consequently, anyone who loves his enemy stands on the same level as God. Precisely because love for other men, and especially love for enemies, is so difficult for us to comprehend and to practice, Jesus came to give us an example of it. Even on the Cross he prayed for his enemies: "Father, forgive them; they do not know what they are doing" (Luke 23:34).

We may say, then, as we look back over this chapter, that there was beauty in the way Jesus taught, beauty in what he taught, and beauty in the way he lived by his own teaching.

At the transfiguration of Jesus, God spoke: "This is my beloved Son on whom my favor rests. Listen to him" (Matthew 17:5). We must indeed listen to Jesus, for then the favor of the Father will pass to us as well. Did not Jesus promise: "Anyone who loves me will be true to my word, and my Father will love him; we will come to him and make our dwelling place with him. . . . The word you hear is not mine; it comes from the Father who sent me" (John 14:23-24)?

On one occasion the Lord said to his audience: "Blest are your eyes because they see and blest are your ears because they hear. I assure you, many a prophet and many a saint longed to see what you see but did not see it, to hear what you hear but did not hear it" (Matthew 13:16-17). Blest indeed were the contemporaries of Jesus who could hear the tone of his voice and the message he preached. Yet we too can hear the Lord in the Gospel and in the voice of the Catholic Church. The more lovingly we listen, the more clearly we will hear his voice.

THE SERVANT

The powers of nature were at the service of Jesus the Lord. "Then he stood up and took the winds and the sea to task. Complete calm ensued; the men were dumbfounded. 'What sort of man is this,' they said, 'that even the winds and the sea obey him?'" (Matthew 8:26-27).

The evil spirits could not but obey him. Thus, on one occasion he was teaching in the synagogue at Capernaum, and the audience was spellbound by his words. There was a man with an unclean spirit there, and Jesus "said to him sharply, 'Be quiet! Come out of him.' At that, the demon threw him to the ground before everyone's eyes and came out of him without doing him any harm. All were struck with astonishment, and they began saying to one another: 'What is there about his speech? He commands the unclean spirits with authority and power, and they leave'" (Luke 4:31-37).

Even death obeyed the Lord. Jesus manifested his power over it by raising men from the dead, and especially by himself rising from the dead.

Yet Jesus was not motivated by any desire for power. "Though he was in the form of God, he did not deem equality with God something to be grasped at. Rather, he emptied himself and took the form of a slave, being born in the likeness of men. He was known to be of humble estate, and it was thus that he humbled himself, obediently accepting even death, death on a cross!" (Phil. 2:6-8).

He whom the angels served (Matthew 4:11) and whose sandal strap no man was worthy to unfasten (John 1:27) was among us as one who serves (Luke 22:27). One day Salome, mother of the sons of Zebedee, came to Jesus and asked for her sons the first two places in the kingdom of God. The other apostles were indignant at this. But Jesus said to them: "Whoever wants to rank first among you must serve the needs of all. Such is the case with the Son of man who has come, not to be served by others, but to serve, to give his own life as a ransom for the many" (Matthew 20:27-28).

We find Jesus' readiness to serve running like a fine thread throughout the whole of the Gospel narrative. As the carpenter's son, he served the inhabitants of little Nazareth with the work of his hands. Then, when he entered on his public ministry, a new and more wearying kind of work began for him. "He went about doing good works" (Acts 10:38), toiled unwearyingly to win the souls of men, accepted contradiction, lack of appreciation, and even slander, and thus carried out with unparalleled selflessness and fidelity the task his Father had given him to do.

Calmly and patiently he served the people. Claims were being continually made on him, yet he never grew tense, never felt overpressed. He was never impatient, never too busy, even though the crowds often left him no time even to eat. He never stopped to count the time he was losing, but remained always in the same attitude of "not for myself but for others."

Jesus served the sick and even sought them out to help them. He had time for children, to listen to them and to embrace them. He welcomed sinners and ate with them, not in order to eat the bread of sinners but to give sinners the Bread of life, which he himself was. As the shepherd serves his sheep, so he served men, especially the poor and the little people. He never stopped giving himself to all who sought him, but shared himself with them unreservedly and put himself at the disposal of crowds and individuals.

Jesus revealed his desire to serve in an especially striking way at the Last Supper. John tells us the story, and we will see from his account how deeply he himself was impressed by the unforgettable event. "Jesus — fully aware that he had come from God and was going to God, the Father who had handed everything over to him — rose from the meal and took off his cloak. He picked up a towel and tied it around himself. Then he poured water into a basin and began to wash his disciples' feet and dry them with the towel he had around him" (John 13:3-5).

In the time of Jesus, a Jew who was not solvent was a slave, yet the law prescribed that he could not be obliged to wash the feet of others, so lowly and contemptible was this service thought to be. But Jesus undertook to do it! His action was not a form of playacting nor intended simply to disconcert the disciples. No, it was an authentic expression of his true intentions. After he had finished, Jesus explained his action by saying: "You address me as 'Teacher' and 'Lord,' and fittingly enough, for that is what I am. But if I washed your feet — I who am Teacher and Lord — then you must wash each other's feet. What I just did was to give you an example: as I have done, so you must do. I solemnly assure you, no slave is greater than his master; no messenger outranks the one who sent him" (John 13:13-16).

As a mother serves her child's life, even at the cost of her own life if need be, so Jesus served us with the sacrifice of his own life. He was obedient even to the point of dying on the Cross. He served men to the extent of shedding his own blood, which flowed from his side when his heart was pierced by the soldier's lance. He gave his life as a ransom for the many. The lives of all men really belong to him, but he did not claim them; instead he gave his own life so that other men might live.

Jesus wished to remain among his people as one who serves. This is why on the evening before his death he instituted the Holy Eucharist, for in the Eucharist he is always present with us, ready to serve us with the same love with which he once died in order to save us and bring us to the glorious freedom of the children of God. In order to continue serving us, therefore, he gave us his body as food and his blood as drink.

Jesus thus became the servant of the servants of God. Instead of demanding our service, he gave us his, and he did so because he loved us. "The 'servant' aspect is no longer explained as a deed, behind which abides the person of Jesus; it is made to embrace the whole existence of Jesus, so that his *being* itself is service" (Joseph Ratzinger, *Introduction to Christianity*, p. 168). And precisely because his whole being thus finds expression in service, his being is that of a son. Thus it is evident that the man who gives himself wholly to the service of others, with total selflessness and self-forgetfulness, is the man of the future.

"If the Master has given the example of service, how can his disciples be minded to act otherwise themselves? If they did, they would be unworthy of their calling and would prove themselves incapable of undertaking the Savior's service of souls" (Tillmann, *Evangelien*, I, p. 207). If Jesus served us, then we must serve one another, each according to the gift of grace he has received (1 Peter 4:10). Jacques Loew, the worker-priest with much experience behind him, expresses the same idea in this way: "We must be a display model or sample of what Jesus is like."

We often have samples sent to us. They represent a little part of the merchandise being advertised; they are small and have little value in themselves; when they have fulfilled their purpose, they are not kept but are thrown away. Their value consists in giving an idea of the quality of the advertised goods, arousing a desire to possess such goods and inviting us to place an order. The sample is not there to deceive or to convince or to compel, but simply to serve; it is at our disposal. It says: "Give the product a trial, test it, use it, judge it, buy it."

We Christians are to be a sample of Jesus, a small part of him that is filled with his spirit and love; in other words, we are to be another Christ, a fragrance of Christ, a sign of Christ and a witness to him, an image of Christ. Like any sample, we must let the world make use of us; we must serve the world.

We Christians are not sent into the world to conquer it and be its master, to lay down laws for it, to force our will upon it in the conviction that our will is God's will! We are not to act like the rulers of this world who lord it over their subjects or like the great ones who make their importance felt (Matthew 20:25). We are not even to let others call us "father" or "teacher" or "master." We are simply to serve as Jesus served, to be the messenger of Jesus, who throughout his life was at the disposal of others. He redeemed the world by his love, which sought only to serve, and he wishes to apply the fruits of redemption through the love and service of his disciples.

Jesus sends us into the world as a merchant sends samples so that we may be a sign of him and witnesses to him. And we act as signs of him not only by working miracles or by showing an astonishing wisdom or by making an impressive appearance which we judge worthy of the great Lord we serve, but by selfless, humble service. He who serves is a fragrant reminder of that Lord who was meek and humble of heart.

By humble service, then, we make Jesus known, awaken a desire for him, and strengthen the willingness of people to accept and follow him. If we are the followers of Christ, other men will become our followers. If we labor in the spirit of service, other men will say: "That's what Christ must be like." If we spend ourselves in the service of our brothers as Christ did, then through us men will come to know, love, and seek after Jesus. Our life is itself a little thing and worthless, as any sample is; remember how at one time samples were stamped "Sample — no value." Yet our lives can become valuable if by our service we show our fellow-men the way to Christ and lead them to him. We might call this the apostolate of service. Let us therefore serve our fellow-men because Christ wants us to; let us serve Christ in our fellow-men, and our fellow-men in Christ. Let us serve our fellow-men as Christ served them, with genuine love and joy.

Langbehn writes: "What a marvelous thing it is to serve! The world doesn't realize this, for it thinks that domination is better than service." To serve with a joyous heart is to bring joy to others and ourselves. According to St. Paul, we are to work for the happiness of others (cf. 2 Cor. 1:24). Let us serve without seeking fame for it, without wanting the world to know of our service, without thinking of piling up great merits, without even looking forward excessively to rewards and thanks. The less men are grateful to us, the more we may count on the gratitude of God, for "whoever humbles himself shall be exalted" (Matthew 23:12).

At the start of the 1870 war, King William I telegraphed Prince Heinrich von Pless to ask him to take charge of caring for the wounded. The Prince wired back his answer: "I will serve, for Christ served me," and undertook that demanding task. "I will serve, for Christ served me" — what a splendid answer! Cardinal Léger, archbishop of Montreal, resigned his position and, though he was advanced in years, went to Africa to serve the lepers. Mother Teresa is spending her life in the service of the dying in Calcutta. Men and women such as these want to serve the poor and sick and bring them joy.

If we serve our neighbor for Jesus' sake, he will free us

from numerous anxieties and temptations, and enable us to grow through our work. When he comes again in glory with his angels in order to pass judgment on the nations gathered before him, he will address those who have served him in their fellow-men and speak to them the blessed words: "Come. You have my Father's blessing! Inherit the kingdom prepared for you from the creation of the world" (Matthew 25:34).

"It will go well with those servants whom the master finds wide-awake on his return. I tell you, he will put on an apron, seat them at table, and proceed to wait on them" (Luke 12:37).

Mary, the servant of the Lord, was the closest of all human beings to the Savior who served. She was his first and best imitator. May her prayers win for us the spirit of service.

THE PHYSICIAN

The heavenly Father knew mankind's sad state and was unwilling to leave them in their distress. Instead he promised them: "I, the Lord, am your healer" (Exod. 15:26). Eventually he sent his own Son to heal men and be their physician.

The prophets preached that the redeemer to come would be a physician. Isaias foretold: "Here is your God . . . he comes to save you. Then will the eyes of the blind be opened, the ears of the deaf be cleared; then will the lame leap like a stag, then the tongue of the dumb will sing" (Is. 35:4-6). Jesus even called himself a doctor. People were objecting to his consorting with social outcasts, with men whom others regarded as evildoers, with those whom others avoided out of fear and contempt. But Jesus, the physician, went wherever he was needed, for "people who are in good health do not need a doctor; sick people do" (Matthew 9:12).

Rembrandt has left us a splendid picture of Jesus the physician. In the picture Jesus stands surrounded by the sick people others have brought to him. From his figure stream light, hope, and help, as they raise their eyes and hands and hearts to him. Some of the sick have already been cured and are giving Jesus their joyous thanks.

Jesus is an *all-knowing* physician. He knew the bodily and spiritual suffering of the paralytic, and in a similar way he knows every human being. "He needed no one to give him testimony about human nature. He was well aware of what was in man's heart" (John 2:25). He knows every illness of body and soul — its cause, its seriousness, its course. What a privilege for man to have an all-knowing physician who never

makes a wrong diagnosis and knows our illnesses and their
causes better than we do!

Jesus is an *all-powerful* physician and often gave
proof of that power. We are told in the Gospel: "power went
out from him which cured all" (Luke 6:19). A healing
power was always radiating out from Jesus. He said to
the leper: "I do will it. Be cured," and the man was immediately cured (Mark 1:42). He said to the paralytic: "Stand
up! Roll up your mat, and go home.' The man stood up
and went toward his home" (Matthew 9:6-7). Today power
still goes out from the Lord, our Savior, when men come to
him and touch him through faith and trust.

Jesus is a *loving* physician. He loves the sick, for
the kindness and love of men which were proper to him
as God drew him to those who were suffering in body or
in mind. He was not afraid of being infected or rendered
unclean by the leper, nor repelled by their oozing sores
— he cured everyone.

The Gospels are full of accounts of cures, for Jesus
never said no. A man said to him: "Sir, my serving boy is
at home in bed paralyzed, suffering painfully," and Jesus
promptly answered: "I will come and cure him" (Matthew
8:6-7). A woman with a hemorrhage of twelve years' duration came behind him and touched the hem of his garment;
she was cured (Luke 8:43-44). The blind man at Jericho
cried out: "Lord, I want to see," and Jesus said: "Receive
your sight. Your faith has healed you" (Luke 18:41-42).
On one occasion Jesus cured ten lepers. In Capernaum he
healed the many sick people who were brought to him, and
even worked far into the night with them. "Good deeds
flowed bright and pure from the deep well of his heart
that was so full of love for God and men" (Meschler).

Jesus is an *all-wise* physician. Martha and Mary once
sent a message to him telling of their brother's sickness.
Jesus answered: "This sickness is not to end in death; rather

it is for God's glory, that through it the Son of God may be glorified" (John 11:4). Jesus knew what he was doing. As an all-wise physician, he knew that sicknesses of body or soul were not accidental, and he knew what their purpose was for him: to turn every sickness into a glorification of God.

A sick man may complain: "I have often prayed for a cure, but the Lord has not heard my prayer." But if the sick man submissively accepts his suffering and endures it for love of God, he is giving God a great proof of his love. He is glorifying God, drawing down God's blessing on his brothers and sisters, and assuring his own eternal salvation.

Jesus proves himself a wise physician in our lives. We ought to be grateful to him and leave it to him whether and when to cure us or seemingly not cure us. What a blessing for a sick person to have a good doctor taking care of him! What a far greater blessing to have Jesus taking care of us! He is always close to us; he never shuts his office; we can call on him at any time, and he will immediately come. God wants us to ask for the doctor in bodily illness; but we should also go often and gladly to Jesus the physician. Let us go to him at the beginning of an illness and even an occasion of little wounds. But especially should we go to him in sickness of soul.

Jesus is waiting for us and sees us coming while we are still far off. We must give him our unreserved confidence and tell him: "If you will to do so, you can cure me" (Mark 1:40). We will not receive what we are unwilling to ask for. Let us tell Jesus, then, of our wounds and weaknesses; let us allow him to heal our souls. The healing of the soul is necessary if the body is to be healed. Therefore, we must humbly accept the Lord's instructions and follow the advice he gives.

When Jesus the physician comes to us, he brings his medicine with him — the medicine of his *word*. His words are a soothing balm and an invigorating cordial for the soul. They bring consolation and give the courage to carry the cross of sickness and pull through the trials we must face.

Magazines and novels can distract our attention when we are sick and make us forget for a while the seriousness of our situation. But the Lord's words both console and encourage. We need only recall what he said of the heavenly Father who feeds the birds of the air, clothes the flowers of the field, and does not forget the worm in the dust, and who cares far more for us, his children, than for these other creatures. "Do not let your hearts be troubled. Have faith in God and faith in me" (John 14:1). We should reverently meditate on Jesus' words: "If a man is true to my word he shall never see death" (John 8:51).

Jesus' medicine also consists of his *example*. His life of poverty is salutary medicine for our greed; his life of humility, for our pride; his life of patience, for our often impetuous behavior. Our lack of love can find healing in the example of the great love shown by God's Son; our lack of courage, in the example of his confidence in his Father; our laziness, in the example of his zeal; our uncleanness, in the example of his holiness.

The *sacraments*, too, are a medicine. In the celebration of the holy Eucharist, the Church prays: "May these mysteries be for us a heavenly medicine and cleanse our hearts of all evil." By "these mysteries" is meant not only the holy Eucharist but the other sacraments as well. Holy baptism heals our soul of original sin; penance heals us of personal sin and strengthens us to live in accordance with God's will. In holy Communion the Lord gives us the medicine of immortality; in addition to an increase of sanctifying grace, he gives us many actual graces that intensify our love, heal the wounds left by sin, and protect us against serious sin.

In his love for the sick, Jesus, the divine physician,

has instituted a special sacrament for them: holy anointing. Through this sacrament he alleviates their plight and consoles them. He does this in various ways: by removing sins and sanctifying their souls; by giving them the strength to make of their sufferings a full commitment to God. Catholic piety has held that when a priest bestows the papal blessing of the dying, he asks that God restore to this person his baptismal grace. What a great physician the Lord is, that he can give a man once again his original state of grace and a wholly renewed intensity of love!

We know from experience that some earthly medicines consist of chemicals, while others are derived from plants and animals. Jesus has prepared for us a medicine drawn from his heart's blood, for we are justified in saying that in the sacraments he is applying to us a saving power which he merited through his suffering and death. In the sacraments the blood of Christ flows out to heal us.

Jesus has entrusted to his Church the communication of his healing grace. Therefore it is with faith and a holy fear that we should receive the sacraments. The Lord promises: "Signs [miracles] like these will accompany those who have professed their faith" (Mark 16:17). Faith in Jesus the physician is not an act of autosuggestion, intended simply to bring one's innate powers into play. It is a channel whereby God's power exercises its effects in us.

The *commandments* of God are another form of medicine. Jesus said: "The Father who sent me has commanded me what to say and how to speak. . . . I know that his commandment means eternal life" (John 12: 49-50). The commandment of the Lord is a source of salvation and life. The more fully a man lives in accordance with the commandments, the more secure his life is. We must therefore make the effort to follow the instructions the Lord gives us, for they come from his loving heart. Earthly doctors are always complaining that patients frustrate the effect of valuable medicines and treatments by not following the advice given them. So too, the sacraments will be of no value to the soul if it does not follow the Lord's advice. Jesus alone has the words of eternal life.

How will I act when I am sick or when my loved ones are sick? All of us are forced to face this question at times, and the time can come with startling suddenness. We will not act properly if we rebel against God's will and complain: "I didn't deserve this! Other people stay healthy, and they live no better life than I do!" Nor will we act well in sickness if we try to help ourselves out of our plight by self-deception, or if in general we live a life of pretense.

We will act aright only if we say with Job: "The Lord gave and the Lord has taken away; blessed be the name of the Lord!" (Job 1:21). Or if we behave like Lazarus' sisters: when their brother fell ill, they sent a messenger to Jesus with the words: "Lord, the one you love is sick" (John 11:3). When we or our dear ones have to suffer, we should turn to Jesus the physician and tell him: "Lord, the one you love is sick," and then leave the rest up to him.

The Lord in his wisdom may not take away our sickness or suffering. Then we must say to him what he said to his Father on the Cross: "Father, into your hands I commend my spirit."

THE FORGIVER OF SINS

How can I get rid of my sins? Or as people say today, how can I be done with them? Many people, of course, pay no attention to sin. Sin, they claim, is a purely private affair, and the individual can and must handle it in his own way; we should make no more fuss over sin than we would over a necktie that got twisted around. There are even people who want to remain in sin; one man said he wanted to be like the brother of the prodigal son and to leave his father and not return.

But such people do not realize what sin is. If we ask those who have sinned — the fallen angels, the first man and woman, Cain, Judas, and even our own conscience — we will always hear the same answer: Sin is the greatest misfortune that can befall a human being, for it means the loss of inner peace and joy, and the extinguishing of the soul's inner light. Sin is a terrible and cruel master, and we must pay for it with death. The sinful soul is like a flower that hides from the sun and does not receive the dew it needs in order to live.

Even though sin is such a fearful thing, we often give in to it. We let it delude and master us. We fail each day in many ways, and anyone who says he commits no sin is simply blind. The closer a man draws to the light of God, the more clearly he will see that he has the guilt of many sins upon his soul. Our greatest effort, therefore, must be to become increasingly liberated from sin and to protect ourselves against it. To this end, we must go to Jesus so that he may say to us what he said to the paralytic: "Your sins are forgiven" (Matthew 9:2).

Judas sinned seriously. His sin probably began with disbelief in the promise of the Bread from heaven, and was followed by infidelity. Hypocritically, the man sought to hide from Jesus his inner state of rebellion. Then when a favorable moment came for acting without prejudice to himself, he sold his master for thirty pieces of silver and betrayed him with a kiss on Mount Olivet.

But now the sin he had committed revealed a different face to him than it had before — a face to inspire terror. At the sight, Judas despaired. "He took the thirty pieces of silver back to the chief priests and elders and said, 'I did wrong to deliver up an innocent man!' They retorted, 'What is that to us? It is your affair!' So Judas flung the money into the temple and left. He went off and hanged himself" (Matthew 27:3-5).

It was an immense sorrow to the suffering Savior that Judas, after sinning, did not return to him who would so gladly have forgiven him and restored him to grace. If Judas had come to the Lord with a repentant heart and said to him: "Lord, I am sorry. Forgive me! I know that you alone can rescue me," the merciful Lord would have received him joyfully and loved him as before. But Judas did not go to the Lord. He went to men who neither wanted nor were able to free him from sin. They rebuffed him with the words: "What is that to us? It is your affair!" (Matthew 27:4).

We will not be done with sin if we turn to men with it. Men can comfort us and show sympathy, but they cannot take away the burden of sin. They can pardon us for our offenses against them, but they cannot remove the guilt we have before God. Nor will we be done with our sins if we despair and say with Judas: "I did wrong to deliver up an innocent man!" (Matthew 27:4). Despair is the worst of sins, for it is the sin against the Holy Spirit and the mercy of God. A man may regret his sin ever so deeply, but if he goes only to men with it and does not repent before God and look for forgiveness from him, he will remain burdened by his sin: "For with the Lord" — alone! — "is kindness and with him is plenteous redemption" (Ps. 130:7).

Pilate sinned. Jesus had manifested himself to Pilate as King of truth and even as Son of the heavenly Father. Pilate's wife had sent him a warning against unjustly condemning this just man. Moreover, Pilate was struck by the nobility of the Galilean and repeatedly declared: "I do not find a case against this man" (Luke 23:4). And when the Jews said of Jesus: "He must die because he made himself God's Son" (John 19:7), Pilate grew afraid. But he was less afraid of God than he was of men and of the mob that threatened him: "If you free this man you are no 'Friend of Caesar'" (John 19:12). Pilate preferred to remain a friend of Caesar than to become a friend of Christ. Therefore he had Jesus flogged and then handed him over to the Jews to be crucified.

How gladly Jesus would have forgiven Pilate, too, and accepted him as a friend! We can sense in the account of Jesus' trial how much he wanted to save Pilate. But Pilate would not open himself to the grace of Christ, and consequently Jesus could not free him from his guilt. After pronouncing the death sentence on Jesus, Pilate felt that a burden lay upon him, for conscience, that incorruptible judge, was more just toward him than he had been toward Jesus.

Pilate could not conceal his uneasiness. Thus, when the Jewish high priests said to him: "You should not have written, 'The King of the Jews.' Write instead, 'This man claimed to be King of the Jews,'" Pilate's answer was: "What I have written, I have written" (John 19:21-22). He was trying to avenge himself on the Jews who had forced from him a reluctant condemnation that was now a heavy weight on his conscience. He was trying to unburden his conscience;

that was why he had water brought to him and washed his hands in the presence of the people with the words: "I am innocent of the blood of this just man. The responsibility is yours" (Matthew 27:24). He did what sinners like to do — attribute the guilt to others so that their own hands may remain clean. But others can really only lead us astray and urge us to sin; our decisions remain free. Our sin is nobody's doing but our own, and we are responsible for it.

The very first human beings began this habit of trying to shift the burden of guilt from themselves to others. Adam blamed Eve, and he even wanted to make God responsible by telling him: "The woman whom you put here with me — she gave me fruit from the tree, and so I ate it" (Gen. 3:12). Eve in turn claimed: "The serpent tricked me into it, so I ate it" (Gen. 3:13). But God does not accept such excuses. No one may blame others in order to shift the guilt from himself. That was true of the first man and woman, it was true of Pilate, it is true of us.

Pilate left the judgment seat and tried, as it were, to slip away from responsibility. He tried to hide his evil action and probably soon tried to create diversions. Many men have imitated him, trying to relieve their conscience by evading responsibility and then seeking peace of mind through distractions or a hobby. Or they try to ease their conscience with excuses: "I had no choice"; "anyone else would have done the same thing." Many today seek refuge in public opinion and try to relieve their conscience through the mass media. But conscience will not be corrupted; we are forced to look it in the eye.

Pilate gave Jesus' body to Joseph of Arimathea and Nicodemus. Perhaps he was trying to gain a little peace through this small act of generosity. But it did not succeed in bringing him peace.

Two criminals were crucified with Jesus. "One of the

criminals hanging in crucifixion blasphemed him: 'Aren't you the Messiah? Then save yourself and us.' But the other one rebuked him: 'Have you no fear of God, seeing you are under the same sentence? We deserve it, after all. We are only paying the price for what we've done, but this man has done nothing wrong.' He then said, 'Jesus, remember me when you enter upon your reign.' And Jesus replied, 'I assure you: this day you will be with me in paradise''' (Luke 23:39-43). In his final hour the Good Thief received forgiveness of his sins, for he openly and loudly acknowledged the Savior as Lord and God. He was the only one to defend the Savior's innocence in the face of the mocking crowd. He acknowledged his own guilt, repented, and accepted the pains of his crucifixion as a penance.

Perfect contrition brought the Good Thief the forgiveness of all his sins and the remission of all penalties for sin. With boundless trust he threw himself and all his sins into the arms of the crucified Savior. Those arms received him lovingly, and no power that hell or the world possessed could snatch him away. Jesus even declared the Good Thief a saint. St. John Chrysostom says that from the cross the Good Thief took heaven by storm. St. Bernardine of Siena claims that the Good Thief is one of the greatest saints in heaven. And St. Cyril exclaims: "What a miracle of grace! Abraham, father of all believers, has not yet entered Jesus' kingdom, yet it is immediately opened to a murderer! Moses and the prophets have not yet entered, and a criminal finds the door thrown open to him! Those who have worked all day long are still waiting, but this man who comes at the last moment is immediately reconciled." The merciful Lord was the Good Thief's hope; he is our hope, too.

When we have sinned, Jesus is our hope in the sacrament of penance. There the throne of his mercy is set up; there he waits to have mercy on us and to take the guilt from our hearts. But we must come to him. We must be sorry for our sins out of the love for the God we have offended; we must form a firm resolution to avoid serious sin and its near occasions; we must humbly accuse ourselves before God's representative and expect total forgiveness from the Lord. In case of need, we can even obtain liberation from serious sin outside the sacrament of penance by a loving repentance and the determination to confess our sins as soon as that is possible.

The great astronomer Copernicus had a favorite prayer which he ordered to be inscribed on his tombstone: "I ask not the grace St. Paul received nor the forgiveness given to Peter, but the mercy the Good Thief received from your hands, my Lord!"

THE ONE WHO CALLS US TO FOLLOW HIM

The Gospels frequently tell of the Lord calling men. The life of Judas represents a vocation lost, the response of the rich young man a vocation refused, while Andrew, Peter, John, and the other apostles are examples of vocations accepted and brought to fruition. Of all the apostles, the beloved disciple, John, has depicted his calling by Christ in the greatest detail. John never forgot that moment; even at an advanced age he remembered that it had occurred "about four in the afternoon" (John 1:39).

The most splendid example of a divine calling is the one received by Mary, the mother of the Lord. In reading it, we do not know which is the more astonishing — the greatness of the call given to Mary or her readiness to accept and follow it.

The Lord's calls did not end with those reported in the Gospels. No, the Lord continues to call men down through the centuries. He constantly goes into the marketplace, among the crowds, and looks for men to work in his vineyard, men to sow and reap in the field of God's kingdom. He is always on the watch for fishermen who will cast their nets from the little boat of his Church to catch men.

He looks for men who will put themselves entirely at God's disposal, true worshipers who will worship God in Spirit and in truth (cf. John 4:23). He looks for men who will not only surrender everything for his sake but will also attach themselves unconditionally to him and follow him without ever looking back.

Every vocation comes from the Lord. As he said to his apostles at the Last Supper: "It was not you who chose me, it was I who chose you" (John 15:16). The Lord may call at any time. He calls some in the morning of their lives, others at noon, still others at the high point or in the evening of life. He calls in times when the Church is persecuted and living through its Good Friday; he calls in times when the Church's labors are bearing fruit and she is experiencing the triumphant joy of Easter. The Lord calls men from the ranks of the influential and from the ranks of the insignificant. He calls whom he will, when he will, and as he will. The stories of vocation are stories of the mysterious interplay of love between Jesus and those whom he chooses.

Many people think a vocation means that a man hears a clear inner voice and responds to it. Undoubtedly there are such vocations, but they are extraordinary and infrequent; the moment is often fleeting and unexpected. Examples of such vocations are those of the first apostles or Matthew or Saul. A word from the Lord was enough, and they followed him.

In general, the Lord calls men in a gradual way and deals with each individual in a wonderfully mysterious way that takes into account the unique nature of each. He does not fall upon a man with irresistible grace, but rather proceeds gently and slowly. Like a man wooing a woman for his wife, the Lord solicits the love of those he intends to call. He waits. He stands at the door of the heart and knocks. When he is admitted, he makes the person an offer: he offers his love and awakens a desire for higher things. He invites and issues a special call, turning personally to each individual. He wants in return a personal answer, for that is what counts with him. The individual called feels that he is personally addressed and personally touched by the Lord's hand.

Through his Holy Spirit, the Lord enlightens the

person he addresses, so that the offer made is seen in all its desirability. The individual reflects and comes to realize, with a deepening sense of joy, how beautiful a thing it must be to follow the Lord. Then the Lord influences the person by his grace, so that the decision is finally made to accept the offer. One person with a vocation has said: "Christ's voice was so loud in my ears that I had no choice. I had to say yes."

The Lord draws a person with a loving smile and makes it increasingly clear what he intends to do with him. Through all sorts of circumstances, as though by so many channels, the Lord sees that his call reaches men. He lays the tracks, prepares the way, opens the door — all so that the individual will come to him. The Lord is happy when a man accepts the call, enters on the way shown him, and passes through the door that has been opened.

In the hour of vocation and decision the person called inevitably asks himself: "Will I be able to be faithful? Wouldn't it be better to refuse the call right now than to lose heart later on and give up?" But he will know what the right answer is and will face the future with great trust when he reflects on who it is that calls him.

On one occasion Martha of Bethany met the Lord at the entrance to the village and then went home to bring her sister Mary to him. She summoned Mary by saying: "The Teacher is here, asking for you" (John 11:28). In every vocation the Teacher is there, calling a person. He who calls is the *omniscient* Lord. He does not simply hope for the best when he calls someone. No, he knows every individual's past, present, and future, his good and evil deeds, his heart and most secret thoughts. Therefore when the Lord calls, the individual may give himself into the Lord's hands with a sense of security, even though the Lord knows everything about him, or indeed just because the Lord knows everything about him!

He who calls is the *faithful* Lord (cf. 1 Thess. 5:24). He keeps his word. He never retracts a call, for he does not do things by halves. He remains true to the calls he has given and never repents of them. The fact that the one who calls is the faithful Lord also means that the person can rely on the Lord's call. That is, the Lord stands by his word and by the person called, giving the latter strength and the certainty that he can indeed fulfill his mission. The Lord stood behind Peter after calling him to be the supreme shepherd and saying to him: "Whatever you declare bound on earth shall be bound in heaven" (Matthew 16:19).

The one who calls is the *loving* Lord. The very fact that the Lord calls an individual out of a great crowd is already a sign of love for him. When he calls him by name, that too is a sign of preferential love, a sign that the Lord wants this individual to turn to him in an entirely personal way. It is also a sign of love that the Lord does not simply command but solicits, invites, and counsels. Finally, Jesus has called sinful men (think of Paul or Augustine) who seemed unworthy of the call; such a call was only one more sign of the love of him who came to call, not the just, but sinners.

As a bridegroom or a bride believes in the partner's courting, so those who are called must believe in the Lord's love for them. They must believe that he loves them with an everlasting love and wishes to draw them to himself, for the Lord will not allow himself to be outdone in generosity by mere men.

The one who calls is the *all-powerful* Lord. The Lord does not show power simply over the forces of nature — for example, over the storm on the lake, sicknesses, death, and the evil spirits; he also shows that he has power over men's hearts. This power is so great that those who are called leave father and mother, house and possessions, brother and sister, and follow him.

Power went out from the Lord, and it still goes out from him even today. The Lord's power enables men to come after him and strengthens them for living their vocation. Anyone, therefore, who accepts the Lord's call with faith in his power and grace has every right to hope that that same power and grace will help him be true to his vocation. The Lord summoned Peter from the security of the boat and bade him come to him across the waves. Peter had the courage to leave the security of the boat and venture out on the waves. The Lord supported him with his hand and did not let him sink.

Jesus said to his apostles — the first individuals he called — at the Last Supper: "I have much more to tell you, but you cannot bear it now" (John 16:12). In other words, at the time when he called them, the Lord did not tell them everything at once but took into account their capacity to assimilate. He did not do this in order to leave them in uncertainty about the future, for day after day the Lord gives his call and his grace anew to those called and thus enables them to gain an even better understanding of the love he has shown them in calling them.

A call is a word of power from the Lord, and a person's fidelity to his vocation is the work of the Lord's powerful grace. Paul says: "He who calls us is trustworthy, therefore he will do it" (1 Thess. 5:24). All believers should ask the Lord to bestow many vocations and to help those he calls give an answer inspired by love. Those who have received a vocation should be proud of it, joyous, and full of hope, and should thank the Lord for the great grace given them. They should attempt to follow in the Lord's steps through fidelity in little things and should pray that they will not become tepid but will persevere in their first love. They should daily stir up a joyful love in their heart by listening to the Lord's voice. As a vocation is received and decided upon in prayer, so it is kept alive through prayer.

THE FRIEND

In the old Romanesque basilicas we find over the high altar representations of Jesus as universal ruler, judge, teacher, and king. Such pictures force us to our knees in adoration of the exalted Lord.

But Jesus is not only our Lord, king, and judge, before whom we prostrate ourselves in reverential fear. He is also our friend, to whom we look with confidence. At the Last Supper, and thus at the very end of his training of his apostles, in the hour when Jesus was giving his Church the Holy Eucharist, the mystery of his persevering love, he said something that gave the apostles great joy, consolation, and courage: "There is no greater love than this: to lay down one's life for one's friends. You are my friends if you do what I command you. I no longer speak of you as slaves, for a slave does not know what his master is about. Instead, I call you friends, since I have made known to you all that I heard from my Father" (John 15:13-15).

At the Mass of ordination to the priesthood, during the kiss of peace, this verse may be sung: "No longer do I call you servants, but my friends." The newly ordained priest never forgets these words, and they remain a beautiful memorial of ordination throughout his priestly life.

Jesus did not, however, limit the word "friendship" to his relations with his apostles and their successors, the bishops and priests; he meant it to apply to the whole people of God. Just as the Savior instituted the Holy Eucharist for all the faithful and not for the apostles alone, and as he prayed in his high priestly prayer not only for the apostles but for all who through their preaching would be led to faith, so he wished to bestow his friendship on all Christians.

We may ask: Is friendship with Jesus really possible? Does not the infinite distance between Jesus, the Son of God, and us sinful men preclude friendship? "How can anyone enjoy the equality that belongs to true friendship when he stands beside him who came forth from the hidden Father, who carries in his person the very meaning of the universe, and who has taken on himself the responsibility for mankind's salvation?" (Guardini). And yet we must regard it as certain that no one can bestow on men such a friendship as Jesus can, and that no one is as worthy of a human being's friendship as Jesus is. No friendship can be more beautiful or more perfect than the friendship between Jesus and the soul. Friendship can exist only between good men, and the best friendship exists with him who is the best of friends.

Jesus chose as his friends whomever he wanted: "It was not you who chose me, it was I who chose you" (John 15:16). He took his apostles and other friends into his confidence, into the school which was his life, into his prayer, into his table-companionship — and into his suffering. He wanted to share everything with them. At every moment the invitation of Jesus goes forth to men of varying callings, characters, and talents. But because Jesus offers his friendship as a generous gift, we speak less of friendship with Jesus than of Jesus' friendship with us.

When Jesus gives his friendship, a man receives infinitely more than he can give in return. But he must give something in return; when Jesus calls, the one called must answer. The first answer is faith, for through faith a man gives himself trustingly to the Lord. The friendship of Jesus, like the Holy Eucharist, is a mystery of faith, and the grace of Jesus' friendship is reserved to believers. If a man wants to draw close to Jesus, he must believe in him (cf. Heb. 11:6).

With those whom he calls to his friendship Jesus *shares his knowledge.* "I have made known to you all that I heard from my Father" (John 15:15). He wishes to have no secrets from his friends: "The man who loves me. . . . I too will love him and reveal myself to him" (John 14: 21). "No one knows the Father but the Son — and any- one to whom the Son wishes to reveal him" (Matthew 11:27), that is, his friends. Through the enlightenment bestowed by the Holy Spirit, Jesus leads his friends ever deeper into his mysteries, especially at the celebration of the Holy Eucharist, at meditation on the Gospel, and at prayer. Once, in a classroom lecture, our teacher, Karl Adam, said to us with great emotion: "If the Lord were now to come to the door and enter in and converse with us, he would not be someone unknown to us but would be closer to us than father and mother, brother and sis- ter, or any other human being. If you love Jesus, you know him." And because we may love him more than we love any mere human being, we also enter more deeply into the mystery of Jesus than into the mystery of any man. To know the mystery of Jesus is to have a wellspring of joy.

"There is no greater love than this: to lay down one's life for one's friends" (John 15:13). *Jesus gave his life for us.* He gave his life for us as his friends, even though we were sinners. He accepted the most terrible pain and the most fearful death in order to win for us the grace of God's friendship and to change us from enemies of God to friends of God.

Lacordaire once said: "Trust is the first step in friendship, the vestibule to it, as it were, while sacrifice is the inner sanctuary of it." When we meditate on the sacrifice Jesus offered for us on the Cross, we enter into the sanctuary of his friendship. Jesus asks the same sacrifice of friendship from us because we are his friends; he expects us to be ready to become a sacrificial victim for his sake. The friendship of Jesus arises, grows, and reaches its perfection in sacrifice, for friendship dies unless nourished by sacrifice. Therefore Jesus expects the greatest readiness for sacrifice from those who are his closest friends; we need only think of John the Baptist, John the Evangelist, Peter, or Mary. The sacrifices which the friend of Jesus must offer for him will differ according to the individual's strength and according to the kind and quality of his calling. Any friend of Jesus, however, must carry his cross, keep God's commandments, and fulfill the duties of his state out of love for Jesus.

Friedrich Schiller has sung the praises of faithful friendship in his poem "The Security." Dionysos, the tyrant, has condemned his enemy to death. Before the execution the latter asked if he might first visit his home and give his sister in marriage; he would leave a friend behind as hostage for his return. The tyrant accepted the security, and the friend went to prison for his friend. Then unforeseen difficulties delayed the return of the condemned man, and he bemoaned the fate of his friend the hostage: "If it be too late and I cannot come as the welcome rescuer, I will join him in death. The tyrant with his blood-stained hands must never boast that friend broke his word to friend; let him rather sacrifice the two of us and believe in love and fidelity!" The hostage friend was just being taken out for execution when the condemned man returned. At the last moment he arrived and cried out to the executioner: "Slay me, executioner, for he is there as hostage for me!" The tyrant was so moved by this faithful friendship that he himself exclaimed: "Let me become the third in this covenant of love!"

True friendship is sublime and one of the most beautiful things to be found in this world. It elevates, inspires, spiritualizes, and perfects all noble relationships between men. Happy the man whose lot it is to have a friend! Friendship is a theme that occupies the thoughts of many.

Now if friendship between men is a beautiful thing, how much more beautiful must the friendship of Christ be! We can rely on Jesus, our friend, but he must also be able to rely on us. The Roman writer Sallust wrote: "In true friendship men love and reject the same things" (*Civil War* 20, 4). At the Last Supper Jesus said: "You are my friends if you do what I command you" (John 15:13). We are Jesus' friends, then, if we will what he wills — the good — and reject what he rejects — the evil. We are Jesus' friends if we are united to him in obedience to the Father's will. Jesus, after all, lived entirely for his Father, and the Father's honor and good pleasure were the most important things in the world to him. Friendship with Jesus should stimulate us to live lives that are increasingly pleasing to Jesus. As his friends, we must make a special effort to avoid sin, since sin in a friend of the Lord is a greater act of ingratitude than it is in others and, consequently, a greater insult to the divine friend.

One sign of friendship is sharing in the holy table, for the sacred Eucharist is the sacrament of Christ's friendship. Thus, from meal to meal a man's friendship with Jesus deepens. Anyone who refuses the invitation to the table of his friend, as those people did who were invited to God's banquet (Luke 14:15), loses the Lord's friendship.

Friendship with Christ also finds expression in love for the Church. Eduard Kamenicky asks those who want the Church in our day to change from a monarchy ruled by God to a republic of salvation: "Tell me, colleague of Christ, what reading do you follow in justifying such a change? You must have Christ saying, not 'I call you friends,' but 'I call you colleagues,' for no friend or group of friends has a right to sit in counsel as Christ's co-equal.

No, his role is to surrender himself with great trust to the love of him whose friend he is."

Jesus does not reserve his friendship to people in a particular state of life, even though it is certainly true that one sign of a love of friendship for Jesus is life according to the evangelical counsels in a religious Order. The religious wishes to carry out not only the commands but the wishes and counsels of his friend. Happy those to whom the Lord has given his friendship and who have accepted his invitation and now carry out his will and counsel.

One of these happy people was Lazarus. Along with his two sisters, Martha and Mary, he had opened his heart and his house to Jesus, and Jesus called him friend. He said to his apostles concerning Lazarus: "Our beloved Lazarus has fallen asleep, but I am going there to wake him" (John 11:11). Then, when he stood at his friend's tomb, Jesus broke into tears, and the people were moved to exclaim: "See how much he loved him!" (John 11:36). Blessed the man of whom it can be said that Jesus loves him! Jesus loves us as his friends if we open our hearts to him as Lazarus did.

Another friend of Jesus was John the Baptist, who said of himself: "I am not the Messiah; I am sent before him. It is the groom who has the bride. The groom's best man waits there listening for him and is overjoyed to hear his voice. That is my joy, and it is complete" (John 3:28-29). The friendship of the Baptist for Jesus found expression in humility, as when he said of himself: "He must increase, while I must decrease" (John 3:30). John did not seek his own honor but his friend's, and desired to lead his own disciples to Jesus. Anyone who loves Jesus does not want to be alone in loving him but seeks to bring others to love him; he feels impelled to do all in his power to bring the world to Christ. In a display concerning vocations I once read the sentence: "The friends of Christ and servants of his name sustain the Church."

The friend of friends for Jesus was John, "the disciple whom Jesus loved" (John 13:23). Jesus gave John the Evangelist three special tokens of friendship: he allowed him to recline on his breast at the Last Supper; he allowed him to be an eyewitness of his death on the Cross; and he entrusted his mother to him. But Jesus also gives us, his other friends, a place in his heart, especially through the Blessed Sacrament; he grants us a participation in his sacrifice on the Cross through the Holy Mass; and he gives us his beloved mother as our own mother. The friends of Jesus are under his mother's special protection and are in turn expected to give special service both to Jesus and his mother.

In speaking of the friends of Jesus, our thoughts must turn above all to Mary, who was not only his mother but his most faithful associate. She was the first one Jesus called, and he took her more fully than anyone else into the mystery of his being, because she loved him more than anyone else. To her he revealed his mysteries before he revealed them to the apostles; indeed, he had no secrets from her, for her love could force him, as it were, to tell her any secret he had. Jesus could say to Mary, and she to him: "All I have is yours."

For Mary, Jesus offered the greatest sacrifice, and for Mary above all did he die on the Cross, since he thus won for her the grace of being so specially chosen by God. Mary in turn offered the greatest of sacrifices for Jesus' sake. So too did she carry out more perfectly than any other human being the mission the Lord had entrusted to her. She was an apostle for Jesus and still is, for her concern is to lead souls to him who is her Son. No one can desire as intensely as Mary that countless men should know and love Jesus and reach the Father through him. Let us learn from Mary how to be faithful to Jesus, our divine friend, and to trust in him without reserve.

A French writer who spent a difficult time in a

forced-labor camp in Germany during the Second World War wrote concerning that period of his life: "It was the most consoling experience I have ever had. Christ was the great friend who was with me at every moment of the day." All of us have had this consoling experience at some time in our lives, and we will have it again, especially in hours of trial and most of all in the hour of our death.

With loving hearts we should look forward throughout our lives to the coming of Jesus as our glorious friend. Not anxiety, not attachment to earthly things, but joyous hope should be our basic attitude of mind and spirit. Jesus, after all, said to his friends: "I give them eternal life, and they shall never perish. No one shall snatch them out of my hand" (John 10:28). Jesus will be faithful to us, his friends, until our death and then into eternity. Therefore we may say with St. Ambrose: "I am not afraid even of dying, for I have a kind Lord who is also my friend."

A Japanese proverb says: "No road is too long when you have a friend at your side." If we walk with Jesus as our friend, we will not find the road to heaven too long.

THE BROTHER

"Mary stood weeping beside the tomb. . . . She caught sight of Jesus standing there. But she did not know him. 'Woman,' he asked her, 'why are you weeping? Who is it you are looking for?' She supposed he was the gardener, so she said, 'Sir, if you are the one who carried him off, tell me where you have laid him and I will take him away.' Jesus said to her, 'Mary!' She turned to him and said, *'Rabbouni!'* (meaning 'Teacher'). Jesus then said: 'Do not cling to me, for I have not yet ascended to the Father. Rather, go to my brothers and tell them, "I am ascending to my Father and your Father, to my God and your God!" ' " (John 20:11-17).

After his resurrection the Lord's love shows itself even more intimately than before, for he calls his disciples his brothers, and his Father their Father. He wished to become even our brother and to give us an example of "how good it is, and how pleasant, where brethren dwell at one" (Ps. 133:1). The Second Vatican Council contains a very weighty and pregnant sentence: "by his incarnation, he, the Son of God, has in a certain way united himself with each man" (*Pastoral Constitution on the Church in the Modern World,* no. 22). All men are thus linked to Jesus by the very fact that they are born into the world. Jesus is their brother. This fact, of course, can be known only through faith. Many in his own day did not have faith and did not accept him: "To his own he came, yet his own did not accept him" (John 1:11).

He was turned away from the gates of Bethlehem and forced, with Mary and Joseph, to seek the company of dumb animals. He was persecuted, sold by his brothers, rejected, flogged, crowned with thorns, condemned to death, and crucified. Yet as he hung on the Cross, he left his mother to us, his brothers, as our heritage: "There is your mother" (John 19:27). His sacred blood, the blood of our divine brother, cried out to God from the earth for our pardon, and it was more eloquent than the blood of Abel. By his death he tore down the dividing wall that separated us from God. Now, in Holy Communion, he nourishes us with his sacred flesh and blood so that we may become truly related to him by blood. In the Holy Sacrament he remains with us as a brother whose heart is filled with truly fraternal love. Wherever two or three are gathered in his name, he is in their midst.

"He is not ashamed to call them brothers" (Heb. 2:11), for it is God's will that he be "the first-born of many brothers" (Rom. 8:29). The word "brother" can be understood in an everyday, rather neutral sense, meaning a rather vague kind of relationship between men. The term "brotherhood" is much used today, and has been since the French Revolution, but it means nothing very profound: "being a brother" in this context does not signify a real personal relationship but simply that people are not enemies; it seems hardly anything more than equality and at most involves the occasional manifestation of superficial emotion.

The word "brotherhood" gets a good deal of emphasis today in various groups and associations that seek to cultivate, through smallness of numbers, a sense of human warmth and a climate of community. People in these groups want to be of service to one another in a spirit of genuine mutual intimacy. Brotherhood of this kind may be a manifestation of generosity and nobility, but it also often risks remaining purely natural and at the purely human level.

Brotherhood, in the full supernatural sense of the

term, can be understood only if we take as our starting
point the basic meaning of brotherhood within the family.
Here it signifies a real community of life, an unconditional mutual belonging, a sharing in one and the same source.
As brothers and sisters, the children of the family love
the one father and the one mother, and in their union with
the latter the distinction of persons between the children
disappears, as it were. They share the same table, the same
joys and cares, the same basic outlook, and the same root,
which makes very special reciprocal relationships possible
between them.

In this description we have the presuppositions that
must be met if we are to take seriously our *brotherhood with
Jesus*. Jesus wished to take us all to himself; he wanted to
become completely human, sharing the experiences of men,
their growth and development. In return he wished to give all
of us a share in his fullness and to make of us, his brothers,
his fellow-heirs.

As he came forth from the Father and was Son of
the Father, so we are intended to be his brothers and therefore sons of that same Father. As he, the Son, knows and
loves the Father and finds in him all his riches and joy,
so we are to come to know and love the Father and find
in him all our riches and joy. As Jesus, the Son, always
has his eyes fixed on the Father, seeks the Father's glory, and does the Father's will, so we, the brothers of Christ,
are to seek the Father's glory and do his will. Brotherhood
with Jesus can lead to a far greater unity and communion
of souls than even the deepest and most genuine brotherhood
between men can make possible.

Joseph of Egypt loved his brothers. When they came
to Egypt in order to buy food, the king sent them to Joseph, his steward, who immediately recognized them. He
greeted each of them in turn, but then his emotions got
the better of him and he had to go out and weep for joy

at seeing them again. Then he dried his eyes and returned to their presence. He forgave the brothers who had hated him and sold him into Egyptian slavery. He invited them to his table, and they ate and drank and were merry. When the meal was over, he revealed himself to them with the beautiful words: "I am your brother Joseph, whom you once sold into Egypt. But now do not be distressed" (Gen. 45: 4-5).

Then Joseph sent his brothers back home to his father with rich gifts and bade them return to Egypt. He sent his father the message: "Come and do not delay. I will take care of everything." When his brothers returned to Egypt with their father, Joseph interceded for them with Pharaoh and won the fruitful land of Goshen for them as their home. After their father had died, the brothers feared that Joseph would now seek revenge, but once again he assured them of his love. "Have no fear. . . . Even though you meant harm to me, God meant it for good" (Gen. 50: 19-20).

Jesus loves us far more deeply than Joseph could love his brothers. "He is our brother, our own flesh" (Gen. 37:27). He forgives us, his brothers, seventy times seven times, and receives us at his table. So much does he love us as brothers that his love drew tears from his eyes (as when he wept over Jerusalem and at the tomb of Lazarus). Jesus cares for us, his brothers, bestows rich gifts upon us, and gives us a secure refuge in his heart. He intercedes with the Father for us, and by his mediation gains a place for us in God's kingdom.

Before his death Jesus promised: "I am indeed going to prepare a place for you, and then I shall come back to take you with me, that where I am you also may be" (John 14:3). His brotherly love shows itself in sharing the priceless treasure his Father's love means for him. St. Paul writes: "Is it possible that he who did not spare his own Son but handed him over for the sake of us all will not grant us all things besides?" (Rom. 8:32). All that belongs to Jesus belongs also to his brothers. He can truly promise us: "All that is mine is yours. I shall keep no grace, no joy, no love back from you."

A mother, burdened with work for her family, also tended to her helpless brother for many years. "He is my brother, after all," she said. If we men, with all our sins (cf. Matthew 7:11), stand by one another in brotherly love, how much more will Jesus, our brother, stand by us! "A brother, a helper, for times of stress" (Sir. 40:24). Will Jesus fail to help us, his brothers, in our time of trial? As brothers of Christ, we even have a right to be heard by the Father when we pray. As brothers in Christ, the way to the Father's heart lies open to us. Through Christ, our brother, we utter our petitions to the Father, and we know that we are heard, for Jesus promises: "I give you my assurance, whatever you ask the Father, he will give you in my name" (John 16:23). As a matter of fact, Jesus need no longer really mediate between us and the Father because as his brothers we are directly heard by the Father. The Father loves us because we have loved his Son and believed that the Father sent him (cf. John 16:26).

Jesus is our brother — not now a merely human brother, but a divine brother. We feel his brotherly hand supporting us so that we can follow him, holding us up lest we fall. Deep suffering and immense love have drawn their lines in that hand. It is a hand warm as the hand of a brother can be when he wants to show love for a brother. If death takes a blood brother from us and leaves us lonely, it is consoling to be able to cling to Jesus' hand, for he never leaves us. And when the hour comes for us ourselves to look in death's face, it will be consoling to know that the Lord who is coming to meet us is our brother. Even at judgment Jesus will reveal himself to us as a brother, for he will say to the elect: "As often as you did it for one of my least brothers, you did it for me" (Matthew 25:40). At judgment the Lord will acknowledge us as his brothers and will not reject us; he will judge us by saving us.

Anyone who wants to enter God's family and into close intimacy with him, anyone who wants to become Christ's brother, must throw his lot in with God. This was a strict requirement in Christ's eyes. "He was still addressing the crowds when his mother and his brothers appeared outside to speak with him. Someone said to him, 'Your mother and your brothers are standing out there and they wish to speak to you.' He said to the one who had told him, 'Who is my mother? Who are my brothers?' Then, extending his hands toward his disciples, he said, 'There are my mother and my brothers. Whoever does the will of my heavenly Father is brother and sister and mother to me'" (Matthew 12:46-50).

Being a brother to Jesus requires that we also be brothers to our fellow-men and indeed leads us to this *brotherhood with other men*. The path of brotherhood with Jesus leads us to the purest and deepest kind of brotherhood with other men, and intimacy with Jesus gives a quality of inwardness to our relationships with our fellow-men. In fact, when we are in Christ, our brotherly relation to others is far deeper in a real sense than it can be in any "brotherhood of man."

Consider that the Church possesses many religious Orders and Order-like unions and fraternities which labor in a very fruitful way for men in need, whether it be in schools or at the sickbed, with children or in the missions. They often serve their fellow-men in ways in which their own blood brothers and sisters do not serve them. And the reason is that in these human brothers they are serving Christ. If a man thinks of himself as Christ's brother, he is also able and desirous of seeing Christ his brother in other men and of loving him in them, without regard to color of skin, philosophical outlook, profession, or attitudes of mind.

If we really love Jesus, we are never alone, for we experience the joy of having many brothers in and through him. Nor are we ever without an important work to do, for we are bidden by the Lord to love our fellow-men as brothers. To the extent that we succeed in this we are the brothers of Jesus Christ. Moreover, if we want to be true Christians, we have no choice as to whether or not we are to be brothers to our fellow-men.

At the general judgment the Lord will say to the elect: "As often as you did it for one of my least brothers, you did it for me" (Matthew 25:40). This is to say that anyone who has shown true love to his brothers will meet Jesus as a brother on the day of judgment. Someone asked Abbé Pierre, who had done so much for suffering people: "Abbé Pierre, who are you, really?" His answer: "I am one who has tried to be a brother." Should not we, too, try to be brothers?

THE BRIDEGROOM

As the Gospels show, Jesus often compared the kingdom of God to a royal wedding banquet (cf., e.g., Luke 14:16). At such a banquet you see various sorts of people. To begin with, there are the *servants*. They obey the orders given and receive a reward for doing so, but they are not on intimate terms with the king.

Then there are the *invited guests*. The king has invited them to his table and thus shown them his favor. He gives them food and drink, but they soon leave him to go about their business. Such guests are those souls that serve God out of love but do not love God alone; they do not strive to do at every moment what is most pleasing to him. When these invited guests have departed, there remain the *children* who belong to the house, bear their father's name, and are heirs to his possessions. They are his joy; he loves them and cannot but love them.

The one closest to the king is his *bride*, and from her the bridegroom or husband has no secrets, for she lives with him in a complete intimacy marked by tenderest love. The union of two loving hearts far outstrips the union of parents and children. She rests on his breast — a symbol, this, of most intimate love. All she is and does is marked by perfect love, perfect unity of will, and perfect trust. We may compare with this the devotion of St. John to Jesus at the Last Supper.

In holy baptism Jesus enters into intimate union with a soul, presenting himself as the bridegroom of that soul (Matthew 9:15). When God wanted to tell men the true nature of his relationship to them, he called himself a bridegroom. Thus the prophets — Isaias, Jeremias, and

Osee — call God a bridegroom or husband of his people, and the writer of the Canticle of Canticles uses charming images of marital love to describe God in his relation to Israel, his bride.

Jesus came into the world in order to bring men the good news of God's infinite love for them. He spoke of himself as a bridegroom. For when people objected that his disciples fasted less than others, his answer was: "When the day comes that the groom is taken away, then they will fast" (Matthew 9:15). Before his Ascension he told his disciples in unmistakably clear terms that his union with the Church is indissoluble: "Know that I am with you always, until the end of the world!" (Matthew 28:20). He loves the Church as his spouse and remains faithful to her, while the Church, for her part, yearns with the love of a spouse for the Lord's return.

St. John the Baptist called himself the friend of the bridegroom, the friend who is glad when he can bring the bride (his group of disciples) to Jesus, the bridegroom.

St. Paul the Apostle carries the Baptist's thought a step further when he says that he wants to present his converts to Christ "as a chaste virgin" (2 Cor. 11:2). Moreover, he uses the image of marriage to shed light on the relation of Christ to the Church.

In the history of the Church we find the image of Christ as bridegroom or husband repeatedly used in religious instruction. St. Bernard of Clairvaux, especially, speaks with great fervor of Jesus as the spouse of the soul. Thus, in commenting on the verse of the Canticle of Canticles, "On my bed at night I sought him whom my heart loves" (Cant. 3:1), he says: "If you come across a soul that has left everything and concentrates all its thoughts and desires on the Word, that lives through the Word and is guided by the Word, that through the Word conceives what it brings forth for the Word's sake, then know that you have before you a bride that is married to the Word and clings to him in a holy embrace."

Throughout the Church's history there have always been souls that have had so deep a love of Jesus and have responded to him so unreservedly that only the names bride and bridegroom can describe their relationship. For example, in the breviary on the feast of St. Agnes, the Church shows her saying: "My Lord Jesus Christ has espoused me with his ring; he has crowned me like a bride" (Ant. 1, Morning Prayer). And St. Mechtild speaks with deep emotion of Jesus as a spouse: "Jesus, Son of the Father's love, wants to be the sole beloved and precious object of your heart's desires."

Jesus, the bridegroom — that is what he really is. In fact, the love he has for us is so deep and intimate that the image of the bridegroom can only distantly reflect it.

A human being's love for another arises at a certain point in that person's life, but Christ's love for us came into the world with him. He lives for and by that love: "With age-old love I have loved you" (Jer. 31:3). Human love can grow weak and disappear, but Christ's love is as eternal as he is. Human love has its waxings and wanings, but Christ's love is ever the same. Everyone who invokes it receives of it without limitation.

Human love supposes something in the other that merits our love. Jesus loves us before we can love in return, and he loves everything in us, so that even our weaknesses and worst defects cannot turn him from us. His love went out to an adulteress; it brought Peter back to him and did not reject even Judas. It was given to the bitter end, so that even on the Cross Jesus prayed for friend and foe alike.

Christ's love seeks to establish a union; it transcends the limitations of human love and seeks to make the beloved one with him. Christ's love makes demands;

in fact, it requires everything from us! It requires the bride to leave everything and to cling with all her heart to her beloved so that someday she may be "holy and immaculate" (Eph. 5:27). Jesus asks everything of his bride, and yet however little she may give him, it means a great deal to him.

The bride must leave her parents and devote herself wholly to her husband. So too the soul that would live as the bride of Christ must separate itself from all that might hinder union with Christ. In the parable of the great supper the Lord indicates the things that might prevent the soul from accepting the bridegroom's invitation: the things of this world (oxen), vanity, possessions (house), sensuality and fleshly attachments (cf. Luke 14:16-20).

In addition, the soul must cling with all its strength to the incarnate Word. If a man must leave father and mother and cling to his wife (Gen. 2:24), so must the bride of Christ give herself totally to her heavenly spouse. This means she must follow him everywhere and in all things, must make his thoughts and wishes her own, and must share his work. The bride of Christ must be true to Christ, her spouse. Fidelity is the oil in the virgins' lamps; it must extend to everything that touches on the person, rights, and honor of Christ. Fidelity must mark the exercise of all the soul's faculties, and nothing may be reserved as being outside the scope of that fidelity. The soul must be united to her spouse not only in hours of joy but in hours of trial, when the spouse seems to have abandoned her.

In a soul that wishes to live with Christ as he taught and requires, the only disposition can be one of total commitment, corresponding to his unlimited love for the soul — a disposition to do his will and to please him in all things. This means welcoming his word, rejoicing in his law, finding nourishment in his commandments, waiting upon him, and looking forward eagerly to the day of his return. It means not hesitating to eliminate all that can separate us from him, and wanting naught but to love him, in the assurance that whatever we may think of as having been lost will be given back to us a hundredfold.

Jesus, the bridegroom, does everything he can to awaken the soul's love for him and to keep that love alive. Above all, he gives his very self in the blessed Eucharist, and through this gift arouses the soul's love and gives the will the strength it needs if it is to avoid everything that could turn it from the bridegroom's service. Through Holy Communion Jesus enables the soul to walk in the light of his truth, in accordance with his wisdom, and under the impulse of his Spirit.

Let us ask the Holy Spirit, who can lead us into the mystery of Christ, to instruct us so that we may understand what love means. The Holy Spirit wishes to fill the soul with such love for her spouse that she will constantly murmur the summons with which the New Testament ends: "Come!" A nursing sister, shortly before her death, said in great joy: "Now I am going to meet my bridegroom!"

In her *Story of a Soul*, St. Therese of the Child Jesus tells us that eight days after she had taken the veil, her cousin Johanna got married. At this cousin's next visit, Therese listened to her telling how attentive and devoted she was to her husband. At this the Saint felt her own heart deeply touched and she thought: "It must not be said that a woman of the world does more for her mortal husband than I do for my beloved Jesus." Then she sought with new zeal to try to please the heavenly bridegroom, the King of kings, in all her actions, for he had stooped to unite her to himself.

THE KING

After the multiplication of the loaves and the miraculous feeding of the crowds, the people wanted to make Jesus their king: "At that, Jesus realized that they would come and carry him off to make him king, so he fled back to the mountain alone" (John 6:15).

On Palm Sunday, Jesus entered Jerusalem riding on a donkey, thus fulfilling the prophecy of Zacharias (9:9), in which the entry of the king is depicted. On this occasion he allowed himself to be hailed as the promised great descendant of David. The whole people was caught up in a wave of enthusiasm, because they were waiting for a ruler who would restore Israel's domination over other nations.

Next, Jesus went to the Temple and ejected those who were buying and selling there; then he left them and departed from the city. A few days later the supreme council handed Jesus over to the pagan judge, accusing him before Pontius Pilate of wanting to be king. Pilate asked Jesus: "Are you the King of the Jews?" Jesus' answer was: ". . . I am a king. The reason I was born, the reason why I came into the world, is to testify to the truth. Anyone committed to the truth hears my voice" (John 18:33, 37). Here Jesus was acknowledging that he was truly a king, and indeed the king of truth.

How did men respond to this claim? How do we respond to it today when the risen Lord lives and rules and dominates the world by the power of his truth and love? The supreme council and the people it was leading astray, the same people who had joyfully hailed Jesus on Palm Sunday, demanded that Pilate condemn Jesus to death by crucifixion: "Away with him! Away with him! Crucify him!" "'What!' Pilate exclaimed. 'Shall I crucify your king?' The chief priests replied, 'We have no king but Caesar'" (John 19:15). With these words, the chief priests, in the name of the people, rejected Jesus as their king, and did it in deliberate disbelief that was inspired by pride and jealousy.

Pilate, the Roman governor, heard Jesus say of himself: "I am a king." He knew, however, that Jesus did not represent a political threat, for he had also heard Jesus say: "My kingdom does not belong to this world. . . . The reason why I came into the world is to testify to the truth" (John 18:36-37). Perhaps Pilate shrugged his shoulders as he said: "Truth! What does that mean?" (John 18:38). To this remark Jesus made no answer; Pilate would not have understood or accepted any answer Jesus could make.

Finally, Pilate condemned Jesus to death on a cross; he did so out of fear of men and as an act of worldly calculation. His main desire was to be a friend of Caesar rather than a friend of the king of the Jews.

The reasons the Jews and Pilate had for rejecting the person, the word, and the grace of Jesus, the king, were the same many men have for rejecting him today. For many, Jesus is unacceptable because to them he is simply a man who died, and their attitude is, "Why bother with the dead?" In reality, however, Jesus is God's Word to the world and the great agent of the divine plan for man's salvation. To reject him is to reject God. It is to press the crown of thorns into Jesus' head and to commit that sin against the Holy Spirit which cannot be forgiven in this world or in the next.

Among those who crowded around Jesus were some who were ready to accept him as king but who had a false idea of his kingship. They expected him to be a king who would bring Israel external power, honor, and earthly prosperity. They wanted a king who would ride in triumph through the world, subject the pagan nations, and assure his own people of a comfortable life.

The devil even sought to seduce the Savior himself into such a conception of messianic kingship. "The tempter approached and said to him: 'If you are the Son of God, command these stones to turn into bread'. . . . Next the devil took him to the holy city, set him on the parapet of the temple, and said, 'If you are the Son of God, throw yourself down'. . . . The devil then took him up a very high mountain and displayed before him all the kingdoms of the world in their magnificence, promising, 'All these will I bestow on you if you prostrate yourself in homage before me'" (Matthew 4:3-9).

The devil was conjuring up before the eyes of Jesus a picture of an earthly kingdom (bread = economic plenty; being supported by angels = honor and triumph; possession of all kingdoms = power). He wanted Jesus to think that if he brought such a kingdom to men, he would be successful and acknowledged by all hearts and all peoples.

Jesus' answer was a command: "Away with you, Satan!" His kingdom is not of this world and follows entirely different laws. In that kingdom quite different values are held in honor.

The devil also tried to fill the apostles' minds with a vision of an earthly messianic kingdom. Jesus often spoke of his kingdom, but the apostles often did not understand him at all or at least had great difficulty in grasping what he meant. Thus Salome, mother of James and John, was thinking of an earthly kingdom when she asked Jesus to give her sons the first places. On one occasion Jesus called Peter "Satan" because Peter wanted to prevent him from traveling the road of suffering. Just before the Ascension the apostles were still vying for the first places in God's kingdom; their imaginations would be focused on an earthly kingdom until the Lord sent the Holy Spirit to enlighten them.

We too are always in danger of being deluded by Satan into looking for a this-worldly kingdom. In fact, in our day the temptation is especially great because contemporary man believes that through the progress of technology, science, organization, and earthly power he can bring an ideal kingdom into existence here on earth. The devil tempts man by using man's striving for power, pleasure, honor, and possession in order to impose a false conception of Christ's kingdom upon him.

The symbol of Christ's kingdom is not the wolf or the eagle or the sun, but the Cross, that scandalous sign of self-emptying obedience even to the acceptance of death. We would evidently misinterpret Jesus' words, "My kingdom does not belong to this world," if we thought that his kingdom really was a this-worldly affair. But we would also misinterpret them if we took him to mean that his kingdom requires a flight from this world and involves no concern except for the soul and eternal life.

Jesus said: "My kingdom does not belong to this world." He did not say: "My kingdom is not in this world." Quite the contrary. His claim to lordship is issued with this world in mind and seeks its verification in this world. Christ's kingdom is in this world like leaven in a mass of dough and like the soul in the body. To serve that kingdom does not mean drawing back from the world and separating oneself from it, but entering into it and changing it from within; it means carrying out Christ's commission to be the "salt of the earth" (Matthew 5:13). Service in Christ's kingdom does not consist solely of the worship and service of God alone, but also means serving the world. We perform that service the more we bring the world to union with Jesus, out of love for him.

An even more dangerous temptation is the illusion that we can bring about the coming of Christ's kingdom — which is God's kingdom — by works in fulfillment of the law, as the Pharisees believed they could, or by the exercise of external force, as many Jews tried to do. No, the coming of Christ's kingdom is the doing and gift of Jesus alone. Anyone who wishes to enter Jesus' kingdom must not seek to assert himself and to assure his own place. Rather, he must stand at Jesus' side and base his life entirely on the truth and grace of Jesus.

Jesus preached the good news of his kingdom to the poor and the outcast. It was in them that he began making his kingdom a reality, because such people were ready to accept it. They were not wholly absorbed in their own activities and were not concerned with justifying themselves.

Let us ask the Holy Spirit to give us a correct understanding of Jesus' kingdom.

Among those around Jesus was a group of people who acknowledged Jesus' kingship without any reservation, who set their hearts on the reign of Jesus as king and gave themselves selflessly and courageously to the spread of his kingdom. To this group Mary belonged from the very beginning, while the apostles and other disciples, as well of course as many later saints, certainly belonged to it after Pentecost.

We should take Mary, above all others, as our model. She stood by her Son's Cross and read the inscription: "THIS IS JESUS, KING OF THE JEWS" (Matthew 27:37). But she had acknowledged Jesus as king from the very beginning, when the angel Gabriel told her: "The Lord God will give him the throne of David his father. He will rule over the house of Jacob forever and his reign will be without end" (Luke 1:32-33).

Mary adored Jesus in the manger as king; she served

him with her love. Mary dedicated her life and all she did to Jesus as her king. She had been conceived sinless and she lived a sinless life; her heart was completely under the rule of Jesus, and in her God was well pleased.

Her heart is a kingdom of truth, for, hearing Jesus' voice, she was committed to the truth (cf. John 18:37). Her heart is a kingdom of life, since she is the mother of life and possesses the life of grace in its fullness. Her heart is a kingdom of holiness and grace, for she lived entirely in, with, and for Christ.

Her heart is a kingdom of justice, because she lived by faith. It is a kingdom of love, for she is the mother of splendid love.

Her heart is a kingdom of peace, because her life was ordered according to God's will. In short, if ever the kingdom of Christ has been a reality, it was a reality in the life of Mary. Jesus became man in order to bring his kingdom into this world, and he shed his blood in order to win that kingdom. Mary was the first and greatest member in his kingdom.

By her acceptance of the Incarnation Mary helped bring Christ's rule into this world. As she stood by the Cross she offered sacrifice with Jesus for the sake of the kingdom. She prayed, in union with the rest of the disciples, for the gift of the Holy Spirit, who would bestow in the Church the spirit of apostolate. Finally, Mary's motherly love promoted the growth of the kingdom, and she was the first missionary in that kingdom. Who could offer greater love to Jesus Christ the king and work more lovingly for the growth of his kingdom than Mary, the king's mother?

Like Mary, we must serve Jesus Christ the king and dedicate our lives and all our activities to him. As Son of God he is king by his very nature; by his death on the Cross he won the right to act as king; at our baptism we have chosen him to be our king. We must, therefore, by faith in him and love for him, make our hearts a kingdom for him; we must by our apostolic efforts help bring his kingdom into the world and make it grow.

That you would extend your kingdom on earth and destroy the rule of Satan: we beseech you, hear us!

THE GLORIFIER OF THE FATHER

Contemporary man finds himself in a very difficult situation, yet he continues to hunger for the fulfillment of his humanness, for greater freedom and self-possession. In order to help him, we must (in his view) implement and intensify that concentration on man and society which the Church has begun and to which it is devoting a great deal of energy. The Church of today has as one of its foremost tasks to give a sympathetic answer to the questions of contemporary man. Man is to be at the center of the work we accomplish here on earth; there, at the center, man does not deny God's existence, but he sees this God of all creation as his servant. This means that religion, in contemporary man's eyes, is not a duty toward God but a means of bringing man and society to their fulfillment. Serving the good of mankind, helping bring creation to its perfection, helping man to become more fully man — there you have the true glorification of God.

But here the question arises: Is creation more important than its Creator? Is man more important than God? Does service to man come before service to God? Does service to God consist in service to man? If the answer to these questions is yes, then Catholic worship would seem to be a mistake, a waste of time, a flight from the real task of the Christian in this world.

In order to find the correct answer to these questions, we must, as in all vital matters, turn to Jesus. Here, as elsewhere, he is our sole teacher and master. Now, Jesus was constantly glorifying his Father, yet this in no way hindered him from attending to men. When he had dismissed the crowd after the multiplication of the loaves, he went up on the mountain by himself to pray. Evening came and he was still there by himself. Meanwhile, however, the disciples were in their boat out on the lake, and the strong headwinds were tossing the boat about. At about three in the morning, Jesus came toward them, walking on the lake. To calm their terror, he immediately said: "Get hold of yourselves! It is I. Do not be afraid!" (Matthew 14:27).

In this sequence of events we see Jesus passing from the service of men to the glorification of his Father; then, strengthened by his prayer, he turns again to the service of men. In glorifying his Father, Jesus set his own soul vibrating, as it were, the way a hammer sets a bell vibrating. In his service of men the vibrations became audible, and Jesus brought all the suffering, distress, and sin he met before the Father in prayer. As the Lake of Gennesaret is fed by streams from the mountains and then pours its waters into the Jordan, turning the latter's banks into a fruitful valley, so the soul of Jesus was fed by his action in glorifying the Father and then passed on to his fellow-men what he had received from the Father.

By his example Jesus teaches us that our first duty in life is to honor God as our supreme Lord and best of Fathers. Like Jesus, we must, by glorifying God, set our souls vibrating, and then, in daily life and in the service of our fellows, let the glorification we give God in prayer send its echoes abroad. In prayer we must nourish our souls with strength from God, and in the rest of life we must communicate that strength to others.

When it comes to religion, a man can easily deceive himself. It is a self-deception to believe that by serving man and the world we have fulfilled our duty to God. It is also a self-deception to believe that by praising and glorifying God we have fulfilled our duty to men. The glorification of God and the service of men, on the contrary, must be united; they must, as it were, look toward each other as the two angels above the ark of the covenant in the Temple did. We must constantly be withdrawing from service to men in order to glorify God, but we must also be constantly returning with new strength from adoration of God to the service of men according to our calling.

Jesus does not teach us simply that we must glorify God. He also teaches us how we can glorify him. Throughout his life Jesus was constantly striving to glorify his Father. In a discussion with the Jews he exclaimed: "I revere my Father" (John 8:49). And on a later occasion, when some Gentile pilgrims wished to speak to him, his soul was troubled and he prayed: "Father, glorify your name!" (John 12:28).

When we meditate on the way Jesus honored his Father, we are entering the very sanctuary of his soul. Within the Blessed Trinity the Son belongs wholly to the Father and brings all reality into relationship, as it were, with him. Then, as he enters into the world, he says, according to the author of the Letter to the Hebrews: "Sacrifice and offering you did not desire, but a body you have prepared for me; holocausts and sin offerings you took no delight in. Then I said, 'As is written of me in the book, I have come to do your will, O God'" (Heb. 10:5-7). Thus, from the very first moment of his incarnation, the human nature that was now inseparably united to the Word was drawn into that mighty stream that flows from Son to Father.

Because even in his human nature Jesus had a direct vision of the divine majesty and its infinite beauty, he prostrated himself in humility and consecrated himself to that majesty in perfect love. No one can draw aside the veil of mystery that hides from us the intimate converse of the Redeemer with his Father as he prayed for forty days in the wilderness or spent whole nights in prayer on the mountain. "One day he was praying in a certain place. When he had finished, one of his disciples asked him, 'Lord, teach us to pray, as John taught his disciples.' He said to them, 'When you pray, say: "Father, hallowed be your name. . ." ' " (Luke 11:1-2). How often Jesus himself must have used these words which he taught his disciples! The words of Jesus to his Father in prayer must have poured from his ardent soul like lava from a volcano!

We can see this with special clarity in the high priestly prayer our Lord uttered at the Last Supper. This was the Savior's evening prayer, as he looked back on his life and summed up what was important to him: that his Father be glorified. It was a priestly prayer in which Jesus, appointed priest for all mankind, offered his praise of God and consecrated himself to the great sacrifice of his suffering and death, by which he would supremely glorify God. That is why he looked up to heaven to his Father and said: "Father, the hour has come! Give glory to your Son that your Son may give glory to you" (John 17:1). But the high priestly prayer was also the morning prayer of the glorified Jesus, for the glorified Son will glorify his Father throughout eternity.

On one occasion Jesus said to the Pharisees: "'Destroy this temple and in three days I will raise it up'. . . . Actually he was talking about the temple of his body" (John 2:19, 21). Here Jesus was describing his body as a temple in which God was glorified. Thus, when he died on the Cross, he glorified God in a supreme way, of which the Temple on Mount Zion was only a shadowy image. Even his cry of distress on the Cross, "My God, my God, why have you forsaken me?" (Mark 15:34), was supreme love in disguised form, a glorification of eternal justice in the midst of unspeakable suffering. The final words on the

Cross, "Father, into your hands I commend my spirit" (Luke 23:46), show the love with which Jesus accepted death in order to honor his Father.

When we meditate on the suffering and death of Jesus, when we listen to the words spoken within his heart as he glorifies his Father, when we do as the Lord bids and celebrate his sacrificial death in the Mass, we should allow our own souls to be stirred to the glorification of God. We must learn to gaze reverently on God, to acknowledge his truth and perfection, to accept his commands, and to offer him ourselves and all we do.

Jesus never prayed for the fulfillment of his personal wishes. Even on Mount Olivet he prayed only for strength to carry out the will of the Father.

We may of course ask God for his gifts, but our prayer is a finer thing when we also give God something, when we offer him our whole being with all that it contains of love, of suffering, and of the darkness that faith entails, and when we acknowledge to him that he has a right to everything we are and have.

The example of Jesus teaches us, moreover, the qualities that should characterize our glorification of God. Jesus' own glorification of his Father was *joyous*. Surely he often used in his prayer the opening words of Psalm 95, "Come, let us sing joyfully to the Lord." A holy joy must have filled him as he prayed such a psalm! St. Luke tells us that when the apostles returned from a missionary journey and reported their success, "Jesus rejoiced in the Holy Spirit and said: 'I offer you praise, O Father, Lord of heaven and earth, because what you have hidden from the learned and clever you have revealed to the merest children. Yes, Father, you have graciously willed it so'" (Luke 10:21-22). We, too, should think of God as the origin and goal of all joy and should rejoice to praise him.

Jesus' glorification of his Father was filled with *thankfullness*. As he prayed Psalm 95, Jesus would meet the words: "For the Lord is a great God, and a great king above all gods. . . . He is our God, and we are the people he shepherds, the flock he guides" (vv. 3, 7). Jesus knew, as no mere man could, the infinite love of the Father — the Father who loved Jesus himself above all else because he was his Son, who loved men so much that he gave his only Son for them, who mercifully welcomes back the prodigal son, who protects man with his providence, heaps countless benefits upon him, and wishes to make him eternally happy.

As Jesus thought of all this, great waves of holy gratitude must have filled his heart. The Scriptures often show us Jesus thanking God: for example, at the multiplication of the loaves, the raising of Lazarus, and the institution of the Eucharist. We, too, should always and everywhere give thanks through Christ, our Lord, as we contemplate the gifts of God to us.

Jesus' glorification of his Father was an act of *reparation*. Jesus often encountered sin, not merely sins of weakness but sins of malice. He knew sin as something ugly, as rebellion against God the Lord, and as ingratitude to God the Father. He suffered beyond telling at the dishonoring of God in the Temple, the unbelief of his people, the betrayal of Judas, and the blasphemies of the Jews on Good Friday.

After the bitter experiences of each day, Jesus was glad to withdraw into solitude, where he might offer reparation to the Father — and how many were the sins requiring reparation! On Mount Olivet he offered that reparation with his tears. "In his anguish he prayed with all the greater intensity, and his sweat became like drops of blood falling to the ground" (Luke 22:44). Then, at the end, his cry on the Cross, "My God, my God, why have you forsaken me" (Mark 15:34), showed how terrible was the reparation he had to offer for the blasphemies of men and the restoration of God's honor.

The more we see God being dishonored and insulted, the more we ought to make reparation to him. Our lives should be like Montmartre in Paris, where reparation is offered for the sins of mankind in the form of adoration.

Jesus' glorification of God was *active* and *authentic*. In Psalm 95 he would pray the words: "Oh, that today you would hear his voice: harden not your hearts" (v. 7). Jesus indeed heard his Father's voice and did not harden his heart. At every moment he did only what pleased the Father, and was obedient even to the point of accepting death on a cross. He was like the lamb that does not resist when it is led to slaughter. By obedience such as this, Jesus crowned his work of glorifying the Father, because obedience is the touchstone. A Christ who prayed all day long but was not ready to acknowledge and carry out God's will and to offer his life to God would not have honored God in deed and in truth. He would have been seeking himself rather than God. Obedience is better than sacrifice (cf. Matthew 19:13).

Our glorification of God must be true or authentic, that is, it must be inspired by supernatural love, united with the glorification offered by Jesus, and directed by the thoughts and intentions of God. It must purify our action of all that is not God. Man is, of course, so created that he can and should glorify God, and praise of God constantly confronts us with the truth that God comes first or, more truthfully, God alone counts, whereas I am from God and exist only by and through him. God is my Father, and I, as his son, am at his service. God has redeemed me, and I, being now redeemed, am even more obliged to pray: "Hallowed be thy name. Thy will be done." The man who lives as God's child and as one redeemed by the blood of Christ is on the path of truth (cf. Ps. 119:30) and honors God.

God is everywhere present and ready to hear us; consequently, we can honor him everywhere and at all times. The inner attitude of glorification is especially required of us when we kneel before the Cross or before the Blessed Sacrament. But we can also honor God within ourselves, for he truly dwells in us through grace. Jesus once promised: "Where two or three are gathered in my name, there am I in their midst" (Matthew 18:20). In the gathered community of God's people, therefore, we can honor God in a very special way. This means, too, that the community is the place especially propitious to growth in the spirit of praise of God. God has a predilection for the honor given him by the recitation of the Office in union with the universal Catholic Church.

In many warm areas there exists a grasshopper-like little creature called the "praying mantis." To see it in its characteristic posture — front limbs raised as if in prayer, and its attitude one of devout receptivity — gives the impression that the creature is praising God. What this creature cannot in fact do, man can and must.

Through prayer, and especially through adoration, man must become intimate with God. Then he must return from this rest in God to action for the sake of God. A Russian proverb says: "A man is most human when he is praising God."

"Extol the Lord, our God, and worship at his holy mountain; for holy is the Lord, our God" (Ps. 99:9).

"We adore you, Lord Jesus Christ, here and in all your churches throughout the world; we praise you because by your holy Cross you have redeemed the world" (St. Francis of Assisi).

"My soul, praise the Lord! Lord, be you praised!

Lord, my God, how immeasurably great you are! All praise to you, Lord! May splendor and radiant light surround you! Lord, how wonderful are your works! In wisdom you have created them all. Lord, all praise to you, because you have created all things.

"May you be adored, my God, for all the beauty you have put into the world. Yet it is but a dim, sad image of the glories you bid us hope for. All praise and adoration be yours, my God, for the hope you have given us!" (Prayer of the Eastern Church).

Edith Stein, one of the great figures of our time, both as scholar and as human being, used to spend whole nights in church praying before the altar, even during the period when she was still a Jew. Her fellow teachers once asked her how after such a night she could come to the classroom not only not tired but apparently fresh and lively. She answered: "How can communion with God make a person tired?"

A priest who used to spend a great deal of time each day on his knees before the tabernacle heard one of his colleagues say: "This evening the main TV program is a fascinating crime story." His reflection: "My main program is the tabernacle."

THE ONE WHO SEES

"Not that anyone has seen the Father — only the one who is from God has seen the Father" (John 6:46). Jesus, the Son of Man, sees the Father; Jesus, the Son of God, looks upon us men.

For us men many things are obscure or even invisible; there are many mysteries in our lives that we cannot penetrate. The greatest of these is God. Through faith, however, we seek to advance further into the mystery of God, for faith is a light to our minds. We put that faith in the Lord, who tells us that he is bearing witness to what he has seen. In other words, we believe what Jesus sees. He sees and knows the Father, whom "no one knows. . . but the Son" (Matthew 11:27).

Jesus is one with the Father and does what he sees the Father doing. He lives in unmediated unity with the Father; he is very close to him; indeed, he is in God, for he is God's Son. The light of God surrounds and permeates his being, so that he himself is the Light. Once we have died, we too shall see, in the light of Jesus, the light of God himself.

At present, our need is to gain an ever deeper knowledge of Jesus himself and in him learn to see all things. We believe what Jesus tells us, for, seeing the Father as he does, he is able to tell us the truth. He looks upon the Father and communicates to us what he sees; for that reason, we accept his word and never doubt.

St. John the Apostle writes: "This is what we proclaim to you: . . . what we have seen with our eyes, what we have looked upon" (1 John 1:1). He is saying that what he reports is true because he has clearly seen it and come to know it. No mistake, no self-deception is possible.

On one occasion Jesus said to Nicodemus: "I solemnly assure you, we are talking about what we know, we are testifying to what we have seen, but you do not accept our testimony" (John 3:11). In his Father, Jesus sees the truth, and his words express that vision of eternal truth.

If John the Apostle can require belief in his testimony concerning what he has seen, all the more can Jesus do so. For in him we encounter the true light that enlightens every man, the true light that is the life of men. We receive the light of Christ through faith, and it gives us security as we go our way. We ought ardently desire not to become unsure or to doubt. "Whoever does not believe is already condemned" (John 3:18). Because the unbeliever has refused the light, he remains in darkness and has no life in him.

When Jesus saw Nathaniel coming, he said: "'This man is a true Israelite. There is no guile in him.' 'How do you know me?' Nathaniel asked him. 'Before Philip called you,' Jesus answered, 'I saw you under the fig tree'" (John 1:47-48). As Jesus saw Nathaniel, so he sees us. Indeed, he is with us. He sees us as he sees the Father, and he sees us in the Father.

This fact should be a source of great joy for us. "I am not alone," Jesus said of himself, and each of us can say the same of himself. As Jesus abides in the Father because he does the Father's will, so we can abide in Christ if faith and grace assure us of his continuing presence.

Jesus sees us. He sees more deeply into us than we ourselves can, and what is hidden to us is laid bare to him. What for us is impenetrable darkness is light to him. One of the Psalms says that God is present to us at every step we take. However far we go, whatever we do, however much we may think our actions are hidden, for Jesus they are displayed in brightest light. Behind the shamefaced confession he can even see the trace of good will for which we no longer give ourselves credit, for "God is greater than our hearts" (1 John 3:20). When we accuse ourselves, Jesus finds in himself and in us reasons for not condemning us.

The presence of Christ in us should be a source of peace and confidence. Moreover, his gaze embraces the whole period of our earthly life, for he existed yesterday, he exists today, and he will exist forever. Consequently, the boundaries of our lives in the past and future are not limitations for him. On the paths we travel he goes before us, and what is still unknown to us has long since been present to him. He sees us and we need fear nothing; we need only call out to him with trusting hearts, "Lord, we are lost!" and he will answer, "How little faith you have! Why did you falter? . . . It is I. Do not be afraid!" (Matthew 14:31, 27).

The gaze of Jesus upon us should also spur us to watchfulness. When some people let a paralyzed man down through the roof and set him at Jesus' feet, Jesus looked into the man's heart and saw that his sickness of soul was greater than his bodily illness. Therefore he said: "My son, your sins are forgiven." At this, some of the scribes thought to themselves: "He commits blasphemy!" But Jesus saw what they were thinking and asked them: "Why do you harbor these thoughts?" (Mark 2:3-8).

The gaze of Jesus is like the gaze of the bridegroom in the Canticle of Canticles — a gaze of love that wounds the heart. In the brightness of his glance the soul glimpses the very purity of God.

Jesus looked at Peter, not with the gaze of blame or disappointed love, but with the gaze of loving mercy. That look gave Peter confidence, awakened new courage, and brought home to him the infinite love of Jesus.

The story of the rich young man makes three mentions of the look or gaze of Jesus (Mark 10:17-27). First, "Jesus looked at him with love and told him, 'There is one thing more you must do.'" Then, "Jesus looked around and said to his disciples, 'How hard it is for the rich to enter the kingdom of God!'" Finally, "Jesus fixed his gaze on them and said, 'For man it is impossible but not for God. With God all things are possible.'" The apostles evidently could not forget the gaze of Jesus. It was the gaze of a friend, and we can understand it because we have experienced friendship.

As the sun stirs and supports life, so Jesus with the gaze of love awakens the life of the soul.

On one occasion Jesus sat down opposite the treasury of the Temple and "observed the crowd putting money into the collection box. Many of the wealthy put in sizable amounts; but one poor widow came and put in two small copper coins worth a few cents. He called his disciples over and told them: 'I want you to observe that this poor widow contributed more than all the others who donated to the treasury. They gave from their surplus wealth, but she gave from her want, all that she had to live on'" (Mark 12: 41-44). Let us try to live in such a way that we will have nothing we want to hide from the all-seeing gaze of the Lord! After all, the real value of our lives is the value they have in his sight.

In the Sermon on the Mount, Jesus warns us: "Be on guard against performing religious acts for people to see" (Matthew 6:1). It should be enough for us that the Father who sees what is hidden sees our good deeds and prayers.

Let us learn from the Savior to look upon our fellowmen, not with the calculating eye of the serpent, but with the guileless eyes of the dove, that is, with kindly eyes that are filled with pardon and make others happy. In other words, look upon them as Jesus does. If we are to do this, we must strive for purity of soul, for the eye reflects the soul: "If your eyes are good, your body will be filled with light" (Matthew 6:22).

THE LIGHT

The floor of the Cave of the Nativity at Bethlehem contains a marble slab with a silver star and the inscription: "Here Jesus Christ was born of Mary the Virgin." On the walls of the cave fifteen lamps hang, lighting the place where Jesus Christ the Light first shone and dispelled the darkness of the world's night.

Forty days after his birth Mary, his mother, laid him, her divine child, in the arms of the elderly Simeon. The latter's soul was filled with joy, and he praised Jesus as the Light: "My eyes have witnessed . . . a revealing light to the Gentiles" (Luke 2:31-32).

Years later, Jesus was once again in the Temple, this time for the Feast of Booths. On the evening of the feast-day a great fire was kindled in a spirit of joy, and the priests, carrying burning torches, circled the altar in remembrance of the time in the wilderness when Yahweh had gone ahead of his people, day and night, as their light. Jesus picked up this thought and exclaimed as he saw the burning torches: "I am the light of the world. No follower of mine shall ever walk in darkness; no, he shall possess the light of life" (John 8:12).

Jesus is the true and only light. Nicodemus came to him at night and said: "Rabbi, we know you are a teacher come from God, for no man can perform signs and wonders such as you perform unless God is with him" (John 3:2). Jesus then instructed Nicodemus concerning entry into the kingdom of God. He spoke of God's love that inspired him to give his only Son for the world's sake, and of the light that had come into the world through this Son. And indeed, "the light came into the world, but men loved darkness rather than light because their deeds were wicked. Everyone who practices evil hates the light; he does not come near it for fear his deeds will be exposed. But he who acts in truth comes into the light, to make clear that his deeds are done in God" (John 3:19-21).

Anyone who, like Nicodemus, goes to Jesus, goes from night to light. And anyone who deserts Jesus goes from light to night. When Judas had taken the morsel at the Last Supper, he immediately went out, and "it was night" (John 13:30). But it was also night in Judas' heart, because he had turned away from the light. Where Jesus is not, night reigns.

"God is light; in him there is no darkness" (1 John 1:5). If we find pleasure in the natural light of the world, we should be moved by it to adore God, the source of all light.

Jesus is "God from God, Light from Light," and that is a mystery that gives great joy. Jesus shines in our darkness, and everything that comes into contact with him stands revealed in its true meaning. He is the true light, and by showing us what he is, he also shows us what we ourselves are. The presence of the Lord makes all things clear.

As the morning sun brings to light both the beautiful and the ugly, so the light of Jesus reveals the good and the evil in man. There are people who have little desire to become better men; they are not enlightened by the light of Christ and therefore do not know the beauty of virtue. A person who does not experience the light does not know what he is missing amid his darkness.

There are people who feel little or no repugnance for sin and little or no need of penance. They, too, are not enlightened by the light of Christ and therefore do not know the ugliness of sin.

The light of Christ is God's gift to the world. Jesus

came into the world to rescue men from spiritual blindness and to bestow on them the light of his truth and grace. The cures of blind people point beyond to the healing of the soul. Recall the cure of the blind man at Jericho. "As he drew near Jericho a blind man sat at the side of the road begging. Hearing a crowd go by the man asked, 'What is that?' The answer came that Jesus of Nazareth was passing by. He shouted out, 'Jesus, Son of David, have pity on me!' Those in the lead sternly ordered him to be quiet, but he cried out all the more, 'Son of David, have pity on me!' Jesus halted and ordered that he be brought to him. When he had come close, Jesus asked him, 'What do you want me to do for you?' 'Lord,' he answered, 'I want to see.' Jesus said to him, 'Receive your sight. Your faith has healed you.' At that very moment he was given his sight and began to follow him, giving God the glory" (Luke 18:35-43).

"The Lord is my light and my salvation" (Ps. 27:1). Jesus the Lord wants to give us his light. Thus, at baptism the priest gave us a lighted candle and said: "Take this burning light and be faithful to your baptism." The reason for the symbolism is that in baptism Christ illumined our heart. Ever since our baptism we have carried within us the light that is Christ. Then, whenever we celebrate the Holy Eucharist and receive Christ in the form of bread, he seeks to enlighten us anew.

The light of Christ is so dazzlingly bright that we can receive it only gradually. Like the rising sun, Jesus seeks to shine ever more brightly in our hearts until he has illumined its innermost recesses and we have indeed become the children of the light.

Contemporary man is afflicted by a perplexity that extends to every area of life. And indeed there is much darkness in man's life, darkness in the form of trials, doubts, temptations, and sufferings. But if Christ's light streams into our life, the doubts are resolved, and the trials, temptations and sufferings are held at bay. "For the children of the light, even the darkness of night is turned into day" (St. Cyprian).

Jesus enlightens us by his example. Thus he says of himself: "No follower of mine shall ever walk in darkness; no, he shall possess the light of life" (John 8:12). He also enlightens us by his words. Each word, each truth he preaches, each demand he makes of us, is a light for our life. Let us therefore receive the light of Christ by acting according to his truth (cf. John 3:21), for anyone who acts according to the truth comes to the light.

We must allow Christ to enlighten us in all our decisions, especially those concerning a possible vocation. There would certainly be many more vocations to the priesthood and religious life if Christians allowed themselves to be more completely guided by the light of Christ.

We must allow Christ to enlighten us everywhere and at all times — the way a church is lit by the soft light of the sanctuary lamp. The holy bishop and martyr St. Ignatius of Antioch writes in his Letter to the Romans: "Allow me to receive the holy light, for if I reach that goal [through death], I will become truly a man" (ch. 6). Ignatius was asking the Roman Christians not to hinder him from going to meet Christ the Light, since, once with Christ, he would be a man as God wishes man to be. In Jesus our humanity is fulfilled and made perfect.

We too, then, should yearn for the pure light of Christ. Our effort in this life should be to be with Jesus, to live with him; then we will become what God wants us to be, and he will find his delight in us.

We must also protect ourselves against the harsh rays of error. Anyone who preaches a doctrine different from that of Jesus is a source of deceptive light and only leads men into darkness. Thus the chief priests and scribes had, by their human wisdom, blinded the people to the light of Christ. Yet, if a blind man leads the blind, all of them will fall into the ditch. Throughout history, heretics like Arius, Calvin, Jansenius, and many others have led men away from Jesus into darkness. Today, through the mass media outside the Church and gnostic catechetics within, many false lights are being lit, and the light of Christ is being obscured or distorted. We must not let ourselves be led astray. Nor shall we if we remember that the pure heart will receive the light of Christ in its purity and that the man who does the deeds of light will travel the path of joy.

Mary, mother of the Lord, was the first to receive the light of Christ. She was to carry it within her and to be guided by it. She indeed walked the path of light and joy.

The light of Christ is also a *challenge* to us, for Jesus enlightens us so that we, the children of the light, may also become messengers of the light. We are to shed Christ's light on those who walk with us. At the very least, we may not hinder the spread of that light: "Men do not light a lamp and then put it under a bushel basket" (Matthew 5:15).

The light of Christ is the light of love. Therefore the challenge issued to us by Christ, the Light of the world, is to communicate to others the love of Christ and to follow his instruction: "Your light must shine before men so that they may see goodness in your acts and give praise to your heavenly Father" (Matthew 5:16).

Jesus wishes to enkindle his light in us so that through us he may shed his light upon the world and seek out the lost silver piece that is the human soul. "For God, who said, 'Let light shine out of darkness,' has shone in our hearts, that we in turn might make known the glory of God shining on the face of Christ" (2 Cor. 4:6).

The light of Christ is also *God's promise* to us. When

threatened by the emperor that "your night will pass in torments," St. Lawrence answered him, shortly before his death: "My night has no darkness in it, for it is all bathed in light." Anyone who lives in Christ's light experiences no darkness of soul at the thought of death and eternity, for since him everything is bathed in that same light.

We pray for the dead: "Lord, grant them eternal rest, and let perpetual light shine upon them."

When a doctor removes the bandages from the eyes of a patient who has undergone eye surgery, the patient experiences an indescribable joy when he sees the light again. What bliss, then, must it be for a soul when it finally looks upon the eternal Light, not by its natural powers of vision, but in the light of Christ! For, Jesus, Light of the world, is also the Light of heaven. That is why St. John can say in the Apocalypse: "The city [the heavenly Jerusalem] had no need of sun or moon, for the glory of God gave it light, and its lamp was the Lamb" (Rev. 21:23). To him we pray: "In your light we see light" (Ps. 36:10).

In heaven the light of Christ will stream into us as the light of the sun does into a polished mirror; it will permeate and fill us. We will gaze into the abyss of light which is the Most Holy Trinity and see the love of the Father for the Son in the Holy Spirit, as well as God's eternity, power, wisdom, and goodness. We will gaze upon the mysteries we now grasp in pure faith: creation, incarnation, redemption, Eucharist, and glorification, along with the marvelous ways of Providence and the history of individuals, empires, and peoples.

An immense and eternally fascinating panorama will lie before our glorified vision: the new creation, the whole world of heaven, the beautiful everlasting city, paradise with the radiant throne of the Lamb from which light streams out over heaven, the Mother of God, and the glorious dance of the angels and saints about God. In that vision we shall also gaze upon the virtues of the blessed, their merits, the sacrifices they offered, the crosses they bore, and the victories they won. And seeing all of this, we shall praise the justice of God and know in Christ's light those unhappy dwellers in darkness who are forever deprived of that light.

In all this we shall not merely look but shall contemplate, which means we shall possess and enjoy: "For with you is the fountain of life" (Ps. 36:10).

THE WELLSPRING

Perhaps you have stood by a spring and watched the bright water bubbling up from the ground. How long will the water continue to flow? The spring that flows from within the earth and never stops, the spring that stirs and sustains life wherever its clear, pure water flows, is an image of the Lord. Jesus is the wellspring, the ceaselessly flowing source of our life.

On two occasions in the Gospel Jesus applies to himself the image of the source: at the well of Jacob and in the Temple during the Feast of Booths. On both occasions his starting point was not himself but us, not his riches but our need. He calls himself a source because he knows we have a thirst that must be slaked.

At the well of Jacob, Jesus spoke of the thirst he himself felt that made him ask for water, the thirst that he would experience again on the Cross, the thirst that made the Samaritan woman come day after day to the well. From this bodily thirst he moves on to the soul's thirst for holiness and purity. "Jesus said to her, 'Give me a drink.' The Samaritan woman said to him, 'You are a Jew. How can you ask me, a Samaritan and a woman, for a drink?'. . . . Jesus replied: 'Everyone who drinks this water will be thirsty again. But whoever drinks the water I give him will never be thirsty; no, the water I give shall become a fountain within him, leaping up to provide eternal life'" (John 4:7), 9, 13-14).

At the Feast of Booths (of which the Jews used to say that anyone who had not experienced this feast did not know what a feast was), the priests brought water from the Pool of Siloam to the Temple and poured it out at the altar.

"Jesus stood up and cried out: 'If anyone thirsts, let him come to me; let him drink who believes in me. Scripture has it: "From within him rivers of living water shall flow" ' " (John 7:37).

"If anyone thirsts, let him come to me." Our relation to Christ becomes even clearer when he bids us drink his very blood: "All of you must drink from it" (Matthew 26:27). "The man who . . . drinks my blood remains in me, and I in him" (John 6:56).

Someone once said to me: "The most precious thing in the world is not gold, platinum, jewels, or uranium, but water. Without water the world would be lifeless." The precious treasure in the kingdom of God is Jesus, who said: "If anyone thirsts, let him come to me and I will give him living water." For, Jesus is himself the living and life-giving water, and without him there would be no life of grace and no eternal life. He alone can quench the thirst of our soul; he alone can water and render fruitful the vineyard of our heart.

Jesus is the wellspring of life through his *words*, for these are an inexhaustible source of new thoughts. In his words he enables us to understand and participate in the beatifying mystery of God. His words cleanse, awaken, stimulate, and strengthen; they create life. He himself promised us: "The words I spoke to you are spirit and life" (John 6:63).

Christ is the wellspring of life through the *sacraments*, for the source of these is the pierced heart of Jesus. From that heart the Lord pours life — his life — into the world and mankind. Streams of salvation emerge from his heart and reach the countless men of all times and places. The seven sacraments are like seven pipes that bring grace to us from the heart of Jesus.

Christ is the wellspring of life through his *presence*. He lives and acts in everyone who surrenders to him. The wonderful effects of his presence are friendship with God, a community of life with him, joy and gratitude, obedience and patience. The world has many things to offer us, but Christ alone is the wellspring of life for us. At the same time, he turns believers into sources of life for others. Anyone who enters into the heart of Jesus not only wins overflowing life for himself but becomes fruitful for others.

"With joy you will draw water at the fountain of salvation," said a prophet of old (Is. 12:3). At this fountain, which is Jesus, we will drink throughout our lives and will ourselves become water-sources that never dry up. The water we drink becomes a gushing fountain of eternal life within us. Through the action of Jesus' Spirit we share in the life of the Father from whom all things come, so that he becomes our own Father and we may call him by that name. We share in his life, which is a life of eternal blessedness.

As the early martyr Ignatius of Antioch put it in his Letter to the Romans, we begin to hear within us the soft murmuring of a fountain that whispers to us: "Come to the Father."

I once saw an inscription on a well: "To give, to give — that is why I live." Is not the life of the Lord, too, one of "giving, giving"? He came, after all, that we might have life and have it to the full (cf. John 10:10). To acknowledge Jesus as a wellspring is to believe and know that only through him do we live, that without him we can do nothing, that our life depends on our faith in him, and that our faith is his work in us. True Christian joy is precisely a joy in this kind of dependence that marks our every moment, our every breath, our every action, and allows us, like Jesus, to glorify the Father unceasingly. Such a Christian can say with St. Paul: "Christ is living in me" (Gal. 2:20). We must be watchful that we go to no other wellspring. We must not abandon the source of living water and dig for ourselves cisterns that are dry or hold stagnant water only.

The ancient Jews applied the term "spring" to the eye. A well is as beautiful as an eye; the eye is the mirror of the soul's beauty, and the well is the mirror of the Lord's beauty. Jesus, the most beautiful of the children of men, bestows upon our souls a beauty that cannot fade.

Heart of Jesus, fountain of life and holiness, have mercy on us!

"As the hind longs for the running waters, so my soul longs for you, O God. Athirst is my soul for God, the living God. When shall I go and behold the face of God?" (Ps. 42:1-2).

THE HIGH PRIEST

In the great dome of the basilica of the Garden of Olives there is a magnificent fresco by C.D. Asam, depicting the glory of heaven (painted about 1720). One section of the fresco shows Jesus as the eternal high priest offering homage to his Father. In the middle of this section we see God, the almighty, holy, good, and merciful Father, surrounded by choirs of angels who sing their song of praise to him: "Holy, holy, holy is the Lord of hosts! Heaven and earth are filled with your glory!" (cf. Is. 6:3).

At the same level, and portrayed as equal in size to the Father, stands God the Son. He towers over the angels and saints, for he is the Son, equal in being to the Father. He is truly God but also a man and our brother who has made his own all that belongs to us men except sin. For this reason, he is the bridge-builder (*pontifex*) who brings divinity and humanity together, and in his person unites men with God and God with men. Through him God reaches out to us and we to God. Through him angels and men can glorify God; indeed, only when it passes through him can their adoration be fully pleasing to the Father.

The Son bears on his glorified body the marks of the five wounds, as though they were precious stones; they remain as a sign of his sacrifice on the Cross. On the Last Day, these wounds, which are seals of love impressed by God, will shine forth in radiant glory and draw the eyes of all mankind to them.

With one hand Jesus points to the implements of his suffering. His hand draws our gaze especially to the great Cross which the angels hold; on it he hung and on it the marks of the nails are still visible. Then our gaze passes to the other implements which are also carried by angels: the cup (symbol of his agony in the Garden of Olives as he faced death); the cords with which he allowed himself to be bound in the Garden; the whips that tormented his body; the crown of thorns that inflicted such pain on his head; the Book of the Law, in accordance with which the Jews demanded his death; the towel of Veronica, on which his bloody, wounded head is portrayed; the dice with which the soldiers played for his garments; the vinegar-soaked sponge with which the soldier touched the lips of the thirsting Jesus; and the spear with which his side was pierced.

The whole picture is a splendid and memorable portrayal of the high priestly activity of Jesus in heaven. Under the old covenant, once a year the high priest, after offering sacrifice in the outer "tent" or tabernacle of the Temple, took the blood of the slaughtered animals and went through the curtain into the second tabernacle or holy of holies, where he carried out his high priestly function. So too, Jesus in dying passed with his blood through the curtain which hid the Godhead from men (a curtain which, in the picture, the angels draw aside) into the heavenly holy of holies, where he exercises his high priestly office and appears before God on our behalf (cf. Heb. 9:24). He dwells there now alive, because "death has no more power over him" (Rom. 6:9), and offers his Father that glorification which has already been completed but continues to subsist in his person.

The reason why the glorification, though completed, still exists in Jesus is that the love with which he offered his suffering and death to the Father is eternal, and so are its fruits. He offers himself now to the Father with the same love with which he offered himself on the Cross. He offers the Father all the glory and honor he gave him during his Passion, when he completed the sacrifice of obedience amid such terrible pain.

In Asam's fresco we see Jesus offering, with his other hand, a golden crown to the Father as a sign of honor. We can almost hear him saying: "Father, accept this crown. It is made of the gold of the obedience I showed you in my death on the Cross, and was hammered into shape by the many blows of suffering I freely endured. I offer the crown to you in the name of the angels and saints and all men on earth. By offering it, I say to you: 'Adoration, praise, acclaim, thanksgiving, and honor be yours through all eternity.'" The crown that Jesus offers his Father as a token of honor is so brilliant that all the rest of creation cannot match it. Jesus gives the Father all glory and honor, and glorifies him in this perfect way for ever and ever.

The glorification is complete and perfect because Jesus is the *perfect high priest*. For he is the Son of God: holy and pure, without defect, not needing to offer sacrifice for any sins of his own.

The praise is also perfect because the *gift* is *perfect*. That gift is Jesus himself, who throughout his life and especially on the Cross offered God his body, his life, his very self as a sacrificial gift. The author of the Letter to the Hebrews portrays him as saying: "A body you have prepared for me. . . . I have come to do your will, O God" (Heb. 10:5, 7).

The praise is perfect because the high priest possesses a *perfect spirit of sacrifice*, that is, perfect love. Jesus could say of himself: "No one takes it [my life] from me; I lay it down freely" (John 10:18), for "the world must know that I love the Father and do as the Father has commanded me" (John 14:31).

Jesus, the eternal and perfect high priest, gathers up the homage offered by all of creation and brings it to completion and perfection. Done with now are the centuries-long efforts of the priests who, in admission of their weakness, could offer only symbolic sacrifices that had no power of their own. Now the perfect sacrifice has come, and after it no other is possible.

How *happy* it makes us men to know that Jesus, our brother, is offering the Father in our name a worthy sacrifice of adoration and thanksgiving! And how beautiful our holy religion that possesses a sacrifice with which we can fittingly approach the infinitely majestic God!

How *consoling* to know that through his sacrifice Jesus offers perfect reparation for our sins, no matter how great and numberless these may be! We do not have to redeem ourselves! We are already redeemed by the blood of Jesus, which makes up for all the harm we have done (cf. Eph. 1:7).

What a source of *confidence* that we have in Jesus an intercessor with the Father! In his perfect sacrifice Jesus prays in a way that is assured of success; to that sacrifice, moreover, we can add our own petitions. When we offer our petitions to God in the name of Jesus, our high priest, we know we will be heard, because Jesus has promised us: "All you ask the Father in my name he will give you" (John 15:16). That is why the author of the Letter to the Hebrews is right to urge us to confidence, when he writes: "Since, then, we have a great high priest who has passed through the heavens, Jesus, the Son of God, let us hold fast to our profession of faith. For we do not have a high priest who is unable to sympathize with our weakness, but one who was tempted in every way that we are, yet never sinned. So let us confidently approach the throne of grace to receive mercy and favor and to find help in time of need" (Heb. 4:14-16).

We hear it said today that the purpose of prayer must be reinterpreted. Prayer can hardly be any longer an appeal for divine help, but must rather be seen as an act in which man gathers his energies together for the task of helping himself.

We know, however, that in prayer we are turning to God. We come before the Father because in the name of his Son we call to him, and he gives us his light and strength. In Asam's fresco, the Father accepts the homage the Son offers him in the form of a crown, and he does so with open arms and loving gaze, for, after all, the one before him is the Son whom he loves (cf. John 15:9) and whom, therefore, he always hears (cf. John 11:41-42). The Father is raising his hands to bless all for whom and in whose name the Son is interceding.

An anticipatory figure of Jesus as high priest was Melchizedek, priest and king of Salem, who, in Abraham's name, offered bread and wine to God as a sacrifice of thanksgiving for victory over the enemy. After this ritual act Melchizedek invoked upon Abraham the blessing of "God most high, the creator of heaven and earth" (Gen. 14:19). Now if the sacrifice of Melchizedek brought such rich blessings on Abraham and his descendants, must not the sacrifice of Jesus, our high priest, bless us for all time and in overflowing abundance?

In Holy Communion we receive in sacramental form the fruit of what the Savior accomplished once and for all.

We should rejoice at the crown of honor that Jesus offers the Father in our name. We know, do we not, that Jesus the high priest is not displacing us before the Father, but representing us? Therefore we too must offer God the crown of honor, especially at the celebration of Holy Mass, which is an echo of the heavenly liturgy.

On the right side of Asam's fresco we see Mary, mother of the eternal high priest, standing in a priestly attitude. Jesus has taken her, body and soul, to heaven with himself, for where the high priest is, there his mother ought to be. When Jesus was completing his bloody sacrifice on the Cross, Mary was there and shared in it; Jesus wished to offer his sacrifice to the Father by her hands, as it were. So now Mary is in heaven at the side of her Son, the high priest. There, with the same love that united her to her Son as she stood by his Cross, she now unites herself to him in heaven as he continues his sacrifice in his glorified state. We see Mary raising her right hand as though she too wanted to extend to the Father the crown of honor which Jesus is offering him.

Mary, mother of the eternal high priest, joins her *Magnificat* to his high priestly prayer. We should learn from her how to unite ourselves to the eternal high priest and to offer ourselves in sacrifice to God with, through, and in him. Mary is the model for the Church as she offers herself along with the glorified Jesus, and of each soul as it offers itself with him.

The whole people of God, which shares through baptism in the priesthood of Jesus, must through faith and love make of itself, as it were, a crown of honor and offer it to the Father through Jesus Christ, the high priest, along with Mary, the angels, and the saints. God ought to be able to say to us what Paul said to his dear community at Philippi: "You . . . are my joy and my crown" (Phil. 4:1).

Mary too intercedes for us. As in the days before Pentecost she prayed that the Holy Spirit might come upon the Church as the gift of the high priest who had now entered heaven, so today she prays that the good Spirit may guide the Church and souls. He is the greatest gift of Jesus Christ, our high priest. "Only with the heart do we see aright," says Antoine de Saint-Exupéry. It is with the heart that we should gaze upon Jesus Christ the high priest.

THE DESIRE OF THE EVER-LASTING HILLS

"Man, the object of God's desire and love." It is difficult for people today to accept these words of St. Augustine because they have lived through so many incomprehensible events. Contemporary man is tempted rather to pray with the Psalmist: "Awake! Why are you asleep, O Lord?" (Ps. 44:24), and to cry out with Jesus, the very Son of God: "My God, my God, why have you forsaken me?" (Matthew 27:46). Nonetheless, if we reflect with believing minds and hearts on the history of salvation, we will discover in it a history of the yearning on the part of both God and man; we will discover what might well be called the "love story" of God and man.

God created heaven and earth, the seas, the plants, and the animals, but he was not satisfied with these. He wanted to create man. "Then God said: 'Let us make man in our image, after our likeness'. . . . God created man in his image; in the divine image he created him; male and female he created them" (Gen. 1:26-27). God intended man to be his partner in a relationship of love. The first parents of the human race sinned, however, and God punished them by driving them out of the garden of paradise. Yet they continued to be the object of his desire and love, and for this reason he had mercy on unfortunate mankind and promised a redeemer.

Men continued to sin and, in punishment, God sent the flood. At the same time, he did not despair of men and, after the flood, even entered into a covenant with Noah and attached promises to it. Noah's descendants forgot the covenant and were unconcerned about God; they turned away from him. Then God chose Abraham for his friend, entered into a new covenant with him, and promised him blessings, numerous descendants, and a redeemer. Many of Abraham's descendants proved unfaithful, yet man continued to be the object of God's desire and love.

When the designated time had come, God sent his Son, not to become an angel but to bypass the choirs of angels and become a man. "God so loved the world that he gave his only Son" (John 3:16). In Jesus' eyes, man was the center of the universe. Nothing was more important to God's Son than to unite the hearts of men to his Father by his own love and goodness. The heart of Jesus would prove to the world that God wanted to be first and foremost not the Lord of heaven and earth but the God of men, the God who took to heart the lot and destiny of men.

God wished to dwell among men and to become one of them; his joy is to be with the children of men, and that joy became evident in the life of Jesus. Jesus dealt lovingly with men, especially with the poor, the sick, the sinful. His yearning for men did not desert him even in the face of the terrible death men inflicted on him. Thus at the Supper he celebrated with his apostles on the eve of his death, his first words were: "I have greatly desired to eat this Passover with you before I suffer" (Luke 22:15). His yearning and love bade him remain permanently with men in the Eucharistic sacrament and to give himself to them there as their food and their sacrificial gift. "He had loved his own in this world, and would show his love for them to the end" (John 13:1).

Each of us must say to himself: "I am an object of God's desire and love. God called me into existence, gave me the grace of being his child in baptism, and has given me so much light and help. As a mother yearns to make her child happy, so God yearns to make me happy.

"When I sinned, he yearned, like the father of the prodigal son, to be able to pour out his mercy upon me in confession. When my soul was hungry and thirsty, he fed me with his holy flesh and blood. He yearns for me as a bridegroom for his bride. He does all this for me, not because there is something I can give him or because I would be important to him, but simply because he loves me. His love for me wounds his heart, as it were, until he knows that I am happy with him forever in heaven. What am I, Lord, that you should care for me? (cf. Ps. 8:4). Grant that in all events I may discover your loving heart and be grateful to you."

* * *

If man is the object of God's desire and love, should not God in turn be the object of man's desire and love? Yes, he should and must. God made man for himself. After the bitter experience of a sinful life, St. Augustine expressed this thought in beautiful words: "You made us for yourself, O God, and our hearts are restless until they rest in you." As a refugee in a foreign land is tormented by homesickness night and day, while constantly thinking of how to make his way home again, so the universe and mankind are in a state of constant unrest, a fever of desire for God and for Jesus, for whose sake God created the world. For this reason millions of years of evolution had as their goal to make it possible for manger, cross, and altar to stand someday in the midst of our world. All history, despite the blood and tears that marred it, was preparing for an appointed time and the coming of the Redeemer, for the world's desire was focused on him, the Word of the Father.

God intends that all created reality should find in Jesus the full meaning and realization of its existence. Since Jesus is God's word to the world, he too is the object of creation's yearning and love; he is "the desire of the ever-lasting hills." God the Father wishes us to focus our desire and love on his Son; he wishes all to honor the Son as they are to honor the Father (cf. John 5:23). Jesus is the Alpha and the Omega, the beginning and the end. The bride lovingly waits for him who is to come, and calls to him: "*Maran atha* — Lord, come quickly."

Every man carries the desire of God and his Son Jesus Christ with him as a heritage during his pilgrimage from cradle to grave. That desire never leaves him wholly untouched. Bold dreams and dark melancholy, war and peace, building up and tearing down, virtue and vice — all are marked by the longing and yearning to find the heart of God so that man may surrender to that heart in love.

Those who call themselves *unbelievers* and claim they can live without God are often filled with a great longing for the God they do not know, the God who in their view must be greater than anything man can excogitate. They search and struggle for God; they are on the road that leads to him, and he is closer to them than they think. They will constantly experience — even if they do not like to admit it — that God is the unknown object of their longing, the ultimate object of their love.

Those who *repent* always find God once again to be the object of their desire and love, and they turn remorsefully from sin to him who, though hidden, knows full well their wrongdoing. They experience him as the one without whom they cannot be happy.

Those who *love* experience him when they surrender to him in love and thus enter into union with him. They come to know and experience what no eye has seen nor ear heard nor human imagination conjured up, but what God has prepared for those who love him. God cannot hide himself from one who loves him, but must reveal himself to him (cf. John 14:21).

The more a man yearns for and loves God, the more God will advance to meet him. The Savior has promised us this, in saying: "Blest are they who hunger and thirst for holiness; they shall have their fill" (Matthew 5:6).

Let us, then, awaken and keep alive our yearning for God. Desire seeks union, and we reach this union in prayer, for prayer is "a conversation with God, in which we tell our love to him we know loves us" (St. Teresa of Avila). Let us exclaim with the Psalmist: "As the hind longs for the running waters, so my soul longs for you, O God" (Ps. 42:2). Or: "My soul yearns and pines for the courts of the Lord. My heart and my flesh cry out for the living God. Even the sparrow finds a home, and the swallow a nest in which she puts her young — your altars, O Lord of hosts, my king and my God!" (Ps. 84:3-4). Let us pray with St. Ignatius Loyola: "Lord, give me only your love and your grace. With these I am rich enough and can ask for nothing more!"

Let us strive to be united to God in love, especially at the holy table of sacrifice. Let our great concern be to avoid serious sin and, as far as possible, all venial sin, for the former kills love and the latter wounds it. We must keep alive in our souls the flame of love for God and try to say an honest yes to God that will allow him to have his say and share in the decisions that affect all areas of our lives. Let us take our duties of state with full seriousness and carry them in the spirit of love for God. Our love for God must, after all, be an effective love and not remain a matter of wishful thinking, as it did with the rich young man of the Gospel. Love for God requires decisions, as the Savior himself assures us: "He who obeys the commandments he has from me is the man who loves me" (John 14:21); "You will live in my love if you keep my commandments, even as I have kept my Father's commandments and live in his love" (John 15:10).

The person who loves God will often not follow the

fashions of this world's children, for one can love God only
if one surrenders the things of this world and even other
people who are dear — a father, a mother, a brother, a sister. Jesus says: "Whoever loves father or mother, son or
daughter, more than me is not worthy of me. He who will
not take up his cross and come after me is not worthy of
me" (Matthew 10:37-38).

If it can be said of any human being that he is the
object of God's desire and love, it can certainly be said of
Mary. The Lord addresses her in the words of the lover
as he peers through the lattices: "Arise, my beloved, my
beautiful one, and come! . . . Let me see you, let me hear
your voice, for your voice is sweet, and you are lovely"
(Cant. 2:10, 14).

Jesus yearned for Mary and loved her above all other
creatures. He did not simply become man through her agen-
cy; he became man for her sake. Jesus, who gave his life for
his friends, gave it first and foremost for his mother in
order to merit for her the grace of election and eternal
happiness. Mary is, moreover, *the sign of God's longing and
love for mankind*. He chose Mary to be the mother in whom
his Son would become man. Mary the Virgin bore Jesus and
made him part of the human race; she is the guarantee that
he has truly become one of us. As Jesus would withdraw
from us if we refused to acknowledge him to be God's
Son, so he would withdraw if we refused to acknowledge
the identity of the Son of God and Son of Mary. Mary is
our assurance that the love of Jesus for us is a splendid
thing indeed and that it is his will to share everything with
us, including his mother.

Mary is also *the sign of mankind's longing and love for
God*. Her yearning for God was far greater than that of the
patriarchs and prophets. Indeed, her whole life was but a
longing and love for God, since the Holy Spirit set her
grace-filled heart afire with perfect love — the love of a child

for God the Father, the love of a mother and a spouse for Jesus, her Son. In Mary, model of the Church and mother of fair love, we can see the love of God in its most perfect and most beautiful form.

In Mary we also see how wonderfully God satisfies man's yearning and rewards man's love. Mary was speaking from her own blissful experience when she said: "The hungry he has given every good thing, while the rich he has sent empty away" (Luke 1:53).

O God, every star in its course, every atom as it joins its fellows, every flower that blooms, every bird that sings, every man that prays, is searching for you. O Lord, all things seek you that they may quench their thirst. Stir up in my heart a new longing for love of you. Enkindle and keep alive in me a deep love for you, and let no sin separate me from you.

My God, how much you deserve that I should seek you and love you alone!

THE WAY

At the Last Supper Jesus said: "'You know the way that leads where I go.' 'Lord,' said Thomas, 'we do not know where you are going. How can we know the way?' Jesus told him: 'I am the way, and the truth, and the life; no one comes to the Father but through me'" (John 14:4-6).

Jesus is the way by which the Father's love reached men, and we thank him with all our hearts for this gift. But the gift imposes a task upon us, for Jesus is also the way that the Father's love has established for us so that we may travel it and thus come to the blessed goal which is God himself. God, who has given us the way in Jesus, will not bring us to blessedness if we do not travel the way he has given.

Jesus is the way. This means, first of all, that we must live according to Jesus, that is, we must contemplate him and strive to become like him. On one occasion Peter said to the Lord: "Lord, to whom shall we go? You have the words of eternal life" (John 6:68). Jesus, then, is our model and points the way for us. He bids us: "Learn from me, for I am gentle and humble of heart" (Matthew 11:29). There is no situation in our lives in which he cannot be our model. He shows us the way in his obedience to God, his prayerfulness, his humility and purity, his kindness and patience. His heart is an abyss of all virtues, a model of every perfection. He has given us an example so that we may do as he has done. We are to *live like Jesus*.

But Jesus does not simply show us the way — he goes with us. He does not simply stand beside the road pointing in the right direction but is our companion on the journey, joining and accompanying us as he did the two disciples on their way to Emmaus. Consequently, we are not to think of him only as a model but as someone we are really to follow, someone who goes before us and in whose steps we walk. That is probably what he meant when he said: "If a man wishes to come after me, he must deny his very self, take up his cross, and begin to follow in my footsteps" (Matthew 16:24). And that is probably how Peter understood him when he said: "Even though I have to die with you, I will never disown you" (Matthew 26:35). The following of Jesus requires that we accompany the Lord with our whole heart and all our love and in every aspect of our lives. We are to *live with Jesus*. Thus, the deepest meaning of the Lord's words, "I am the way," is to live in Christ.

Christ is not only the way; he is also the truth and the life. He is both goal and way to it. In Jesus, God provides the way but also the strength to travel that way to him. Without Jesus we would not know how to reach the Father, and if we did know it, we would not have the strength to reach him. Jesus shows us that the Father is our goal; he leads us, even carries us, to that goal.

Jesus the Way is also life and the vital power to travel the way. His Spirit urges us forward on the way to God.

Pascal somewhere speaks of rivers as "ways that themselves move and lead a man to where he wants to go." Jesus is such a road. He carries us to our goal, as the water of the river carries a man in his boat.

If Jesus is in us, we feel ourselves drawn and supported by him in the recesses of our souls. His presence means that the goal of our life is already within us, and his Spirit in us enables us to bring the life of Jesus in us to its perfect form. As plants have an interior principle that enables them to develop to their full form, so the Spirit of Jesus, whom we have received in baptism, is a principle within us enabling us to develop to its full form the life proper to the children of God. We possess the Spirit of adoption, by whose power we cry out: "*Abba*, dear Father!"

We men of today live in a different age and a different world than Jesus did. It is impossible, therefore, for us to live in our industrial society exactly as Jesus and the apostles lived in their time. But if Jesus lives in us through the Spirit who makes us children of God, and if we live in Jesus, we can live today a life that is holy and pleasing to God. The externals may have changed, but the spirit remains the same.

We are, therefore, to *live in Jesus* by allowing ourselves to be guided by love for him and energized by his grace. If Jesus is really to live in us, we must allow ourselves to be formed by him and must create an even larger space for him within us by frequently receiving the sacraments of penance and the Eucharist. We must never allow his Spirit to be quenched in us by serious sin.

Travelers who want to cover a long distance leave behind all unnecessary burdens. As travelers to God, we must leave behind all that can hinder us from moving forward; we must leave behind, in short, our dependence on the material things and joys and honors of this world.

Jesus was the way for Mary and the saints; he is still the way for the countless men and women in whom he lives and acts. He must be your way and your life, too. If we are to reach the road which Jesus is, there must be access roads. The best, surest, and shortest of these is Mary. There is no better way for us to reach Jesus.

THE VINE

In the parable of the laborers in the vineyard (Matthew 20:1-16), Jesus tells how an estate owner went out to hire laborers for his vineyard. He hired men at dawn, midmorning, noon, and midafternoon. Then in late afternoon, around five o'clock, he went out and found still others standing idle in the marketplace. To these he said: "You too go along to my vineyard and I will pay you whatever is fair."

Jesus is the master; we are the workers. He sends us into his vineyard, which is the Church but also our own souls. However, we are not simply workers in the Lord's vineyard. We are ourselves the *vineyard* that he has laid out with special care and love. Consequently, what the prophet Isaias is bidden by God to say about God's people, Israel, we should apply to the Church and our souls: "Let me now sing of my friend, my friend's song concerning his vineyard. My friend had a vineyard on a fertile hillside; he spaded it, cleared it of stones, and planted the choicest vines; within it he built a watchtower and hewed out a wine press. Then he looked for the crop of grapes. . . . What more was there to do for my vineyard that I had not done?" (Is. 5:1-4).

The relation of Jesus to us, however, is not quite like that of the owner to the vineyard. His relation to us is far more intimate and is rather like that of the vine to its branches.

In baptism, we became *branches* on the vine which is Christ, and we must remain united to him as branches to the vine. Jesus says in his explanation of the relationship: "I am the vine, you are the branches. He who lives in me and I in him, will produce abundantly, for apart from me you can do nothing" (John 15:5). Without Jesus we can do nothing. St. Augustine comments: "He does not say that without him we cannot do difficult things or that without him we can do only a little good. No, without him we can do absolutely nothing that is good."

But Jesus is not only the one without whom we can do nothing. He is also the one who makes all things possible. Abbé Huvelin puts it this way: "If a soul loses courage despite the Eucharist, it blasphemes." He says this because our life in Christ is accompanied by the assurance of God's unlimited generosity. The person who loves Jesus is not just drawn by him as though he were standing at a distance; no, he is drawn into the Mystical Body of Jesus as nourishment is drawn up into the vine. He is now at the disposal of the Spirit, who is the soul of the Mystical Body and will form this person and make him produce fruit that is far beyond his own inherent powers.

The smallest act or movement of the will that is according to God's will and does him honor is the work of Jesus within us. Consequently, it must be our primary concern to remain in the love of Jesus. "You are the branches. . . . It was I who chose you to go forth and bear fruit" (John 15:5, 16); "My Father has been glorified in your bearing much fruit and becoming my disciples" (John 15:8).

We must produce fruit. We resemble a fruitful branch if we remain in Christ, that is, if we live in sanctifying grace and avoid serious sin. We resemble a shriveling branch if venial sins crack and weaken our links with the vine, for then the channels of grace get blocked up. The fruits brought forth by a cracked or sick branch are few and far between, and such as do appear are neither sweet nor good to look at.

Finally, we resemble a completely withered branch when serious sin separates us from Jesus, for then the Lord's

words have their full application: "Apart from me you can
do nothing." The lack of fruit is a sign that the vital connection with Jesus has been broken, and that is a dangerous
situation for any Christian to be in.

We keep the connection with Jesus what it should be
through prayer and especially through the reception of the
Bread of life. Does Jesus not promise: "If you do not eat
the flesh of the Son of Man and drink his blood, you have
no life in you. He who feeds on my flesh and drinks my
blood has life eternal" (John 6:53-54)? Without the union
with Jesus which the reception of his body and blood makes
possible, we would be a withered vine that is thrown into
the fire because it is good for nothing.

We must let ourselves be purified so that we may bring
forth greater fruit. The vinegrower who does the pruning
is the Father (John 15:1). He tests our thinking and our
action. Everything not directed to the purpose of bringing
forth fruit displeases him, and he wants to remove it from
our lives. Sometimes he accomplishes his purpose through
remorse of conscience, which cuts into the soul like a sharp
pruning knife and removes the parasites that bear no fruit.
At other times God uses stronger means of pruning — suffering and trials. The man of faith sees in these the loving
hand of the heavenly Vinegrower.

We must not try to seize God's arms and hold him
back, but rather let him work in peace. Nor should we complain about his action or bother him with prayers to stop
this pruning that is inspired by love. He will never cut too
deeply or too quickly or too extensively. We should rather,
then, think often of the heavenly Vinegrower at his work,
feel joy at his presence, and ask him to carry his love-inspired
work to completion in us.

The vinegrower does not allow branches to grow
directly out of the ground, for they do not have the power
of the oak tree to rise upward. Instead, he grafts them on

to the stock. So too the heavenly Vinegrower grafts our life to the stock of the Cross, which his loving wisdom brought into existence. It is a grafting filled with the promise of happiness, since it is God's work and forces the vine to grow tall.

The Father is the Vinegrower for the Church as well. He is always with her, always taking care of her. He purifies and sanctifies her so that she may always be fruitful.

God, our heavenly Father, you are the Vinegrower. Through your Son you have planted the heavenly vine on our earth so that by means of it we may share in your divine life. That all men may become branches of the heavenly vine: we beseech you, hear us!

Purify us so that we may bring forth greater fruit. Grant us at all times your loving help and protection. Grant that at the end of our lives we may not be fruitless branches, but rather let us all remain united to you in truth, love, and grace.

THE BREAD

In the evening, after the miraculous multiplication of loaves, Jesus withdrew to the mountain alone. His disciples, meanwhile, he sent back to Capernaum. As they crossed the sea during the night, the wind turned against them, and by midnight they were still only halfway to their destination. Jesus knew of their difficult situation and, in order to help them, left his solitude and prayer and came to them walking on the waters. Rejoicing, they took him into the boat, and soon the boat came aground on the shore to which they had been heading.

Early in the morning Jesus went to the synagogue at Capernaum to instruct the people. There he found the same people he had fed in the deserted place the day before. "They said to him, 'Rabbi, when did you come here?' Jesus answered them: 'I assure you, you are not looking for me because you have seen signs but because you have eaten your fill of the loaves. You should not be working for perishable food but for food that remains unto life eternal, food which the Son of Man will give you; it is on him that God the Father has set his seal'" (John 6:25-27).

Hunger for food had brought the people to Jesus again, for hunger has power to drive men. To satisfy their hunger, men make great efforts; they work. When hunger is satisfied, men have a sense of well-being and even of joy; in fact, a meal is a definite means of producing joy.

Now, Jesus knew that it is not for bodily food alone that men hunger. That was why he said to these people: "You are not looking for me because you have seen signs but because you have eaten your fill of the loaves. You should not be working for perishable food" (John 6:26-27). Earthly food is perishable and imperfect, just as the earthly life it supports is perishable and incomplete. Earthly bread cannot really bestow life; it can only sustain a life already given by restoring energies used up in daily life. Even then earthly food cannot indefinitely preserve life. As the Jews who ate the manna in the desert died, so men must die no matter how much bodily food they may have.

After the fall, God said to Adam: "Cursed be the ground because of you! In toil shall you eat its yield all the days of your life" (Gen. 3:17). Thus, since the fall, food itself is to some extent a means of punishment and death, simply because it must be brought forth through heavy toil from the cursed earth and so causes man affliction and even servitude. How often we see men thus punished in the places where they must do heavy work!

But man does not have only a transitory life; he also has a life that is permanent and divine in character. To support this life he needs a food that contains divine life and supplies him with that life. That is the bread of which Jesus is speaking when he says that his hearers should be working "for food that remains unto life eternal." It has pleased God that we should share his very nature and should become the heirs of his own riches and eternal happiness. He has willed that his Spirit should introduce us to the depths of his life.

And the way he has chosen for bringing us to this goal is no less astounding than the goal itself. That way is Jesus. He is the way by which men reach the Father, are united to him, and come to share his life. Through Jesus they begin to live in God, just as Jesus lives in his Father. Through Jesus they acquire the Spirit of the Father and the Son. Jesus himself points the way for them, for in his person they discover the law they must follow in their lives and the teaching they need if they are truly to live as God's children.

Those who believe and come to Jesus and receive

him as the Bread of life thereby have access to the Father. With Jesus they cross the mysterious threshold of the temple in which God dwells. For when they eat Jesus, the Bread from heaven, they prove the truth of his words: "I myself am the living bread come down from heaven. If anyone eats this bread he shall live forever; the bread I will give is my flesh, for the life of the world" (John 6:51). He is the food that remains unto life eternal. For the bread that men are to receive is not simply a gift from Jesus — it is Jesus himself.

The Jews asked one another: "How can he give us his flesh to eat?" Jesus told them: "He who feeds on my flesh and drinks my blood has life eternal" (John 6:52, 54). He also promised that "the man who feeds on me will have life because of me" (John 6:57). The food that Jesus gives is his body that will be offered in sacrifice and his blood that will be poured out. The meal he offers men is a memorial and the ongoing presence of his self-sacrifice. It makes believers sharers in his suffering; it gives them the strength to live his crucifixion with him by putting to death their passions and their distorted hunger for life as they live out their lives in the midst of a world dominated by the pursuit of pleasure yet also full of suffering.

The man who eats the food that Jesus gives will live for the sake of the Father. The living Father had sent Jesus, and Jesus lived for the Father. The man who eats Jesus will do the same. Thus every celebration of the Eucharistic meal is, for the Christian, an acceptance with Jesus of the Father's will. He becomes one with Jesus and his "giving of thanks"; he celebrates the meal as a joyous thanksgiving for everything, and especially for God's action in saving mankind.

"The man who feeds on this bread shall live forever" (John 6:58). Anyone who receives Jesus remains united to him even in death, for Jesus promises: "I will raise him up on the last day" (John 6:54).

The Eucharistic meal is also a memorial of the resurrection and return of Jesus. The one who remains in Jesus and in whom Jesus remains has the power to live even now on earth a life that is transfigured, a life that is no longer dominated by the lust for what this world has to offer, but is filled with an interior joy. His life already contains in germ the happiness of heaven, and someday it will flower and produce the fruit of eternal blessedness.

Man cannot obtain earthly food without toil. So too, the Christian cannot obtain the Bread of heaven, the Bread of eternal life, without working for it. The Jews surmised this, and therefore asked Jesus: "What must we do to perform the works of God?" (John 6:28). They were asking, in effect: "What work must we do for God in order to win this food?" Jesus then answered: "This is the work of God: have faith in the One whom he sent" (John 6:29). The crucial thing, then, is to accept Jesus into our lives through faith, to imitate his life in the living of our earthly life, and thus to gain through him a share in eternal life. The work required of us is to believe in the word of Jesus and to come to know him as he really is. Our work is to let God instruct us through Jesus' word and determine how we are to live. The Father draws us to the Son.

Our model in all this is Mary, whom her cousin Elizabeth called blessed because of her faith (Luke 1:45). Her faith was not vision but authentic faith, and it became the very foundation of her life. Because Mary believed so perfectly in the Redeemer, she became, in accordance with God's plan, the mother of his Son. The testing of the faith of this woman who was God's mother took place every day of her life, for that life took her, at the side of Jesus, her divine Son, not to the heights of earthly glory but from the manger to the Cross.

Mary lived by faith in Jesus. In the "Hail, Holy Queen," we turn to God's mother with the prayer: "Show unto us the blessed fruit of thy womb, Jesus!" That is the prayer we ought constantly be directing to Mary, for every mother likes to show her child, and Mary is no different. She wishes to present her Son to us and to tell us that he is the Bread of life for us. After her Son had ascended to his Father, Mary herself received the Bread of life from the hand of St. John and thus remained united with her Son in spirit, even more closely than she had earlier been united to him in body. In the Eucharist she celebrated the death of her Son until he should come again and take her to share his glory.

Mary is thus our model, especially in celebrating the Eucharist. We may note that nowhere do people enter more deeply into the celebration of Jesus' death in the Mass, nowhere do they receive the Bread of heaven more frequently and with greater piety than at the pilgrimage shrines of Mary.

THE FIRE

An ancient myth tells of Prometheus, a son of the gods, who took fire from heaven and gave it to men on earth. The angry gods punished him by chaining him to a peak in the Caucasus.

Jesus, the Son of God, came to us on earth and brought us the fire of holy love. For this, the very men to whom he had brought this sacred fire, nailed him to a cross. But their action did not quench the fire, but on the contrary caused it to flame out irresistibly.

In the cathedral of Wuerzburg, where ordinations to the priesthood and religious professions take place each year, I saw a tabernacle which especially attracted my attention. I shall not soon forget it, so great is its power of artistic expression. It is carved in stone in the form of a burning flame, in the midst of which the Blessed Sacrament is reserved. The flickering light of a small sanctuary lamp plays over the stone.

When I saw the tabernacle, I remembered the Lord's words: "I have come to light a fire on the earth. How I wish the blaze were ignited!" (Luke 12:49) and the invocation in the litany: "Heart of Jesus, burning furnace of charity, have mercy on us!"

In the heart of Jesus, present in the Blessed Sacrament, there burns a double flame of love. There is, first of all, *love for the Father*. This love filled the heart of Jesus from the very first moment of the Incarnation. It caused him to be consumed with zeal for his Father's honor; it led him to the sacrifice of the Cross, for, as he said of himself: "No one takes it [my life] from me. I lay it down freely. . . . The world must know that I love the Father and do as the Father has commanded me" (John 10:18 and 14:31).

In the heart of Jesus there also burns a *love for us men*. He indicated this when he said: "There is no greater love than this: to lay down one's life for one's friends" (John 15:13). Jesus allowed his heart to be opened. The blood and water that flowed from it were a sign of the Holy Spirit (the very Love of Jesus and the Father for each other) being poured out upon us, so that we might be aware of this divine love that is shown us and might realize that "God is love" (1 John 4:8). To the love of Jesus for us, then, we should entrust all our petitions and desires.

But Jesus wants the love in his heart to burn in ours as well. He wants our hearts, too, to become furnaces of love for the Father and for men. Our love should not be a poor little spark! Our hearts should be furnaces filled with bright flames that shed their light on all around us.

In wooded areas we can even today still find charcoal kilns. The owner puts layers of wood on the fire and covers the whole pile with a layer of earth; then he lights it. He keeps watch so that the flames do not burst out at any point. The whole pile must simply burn within and give off smoke. These kilns are built out in the woods but cause no forest fires.

Our lives as Christians should not resemble the smoldering, smoking fires of the charcoal kilns. In us there should rather be a fire that leaps out to seize on what is near it. If we are truly on fire, we must set others ablaze. But how can such a fire be kindled in us?

Jesus is "a consuming fire" (Heb. 12:29). We must therefore draw near to him and let his flame set us afire.

We draw near in prayer. When we pray, God gladly casts into our hearts a spark of holy love.

We draw near especially in the Holy Eucharist. When we adore and receive the sacrament of love, our souls are inflamed with love of both the all-holy God and our fellowmen. The Blessed Sacrament not only kindles love; it also sustains, feeds, and strengthens it. Moreover, it is not simply priests and religious but all the faithful that should allow the fire in the tabernacle to be kindled in them. They must let Jesus baptize them with fire. The word "baptism" means to dip or immerse. All the faithful must be dipped in, even immersed in, the fire of Jesus' love, so that it will permeate their whole being. The fire of love must burn away everything in us that can be a barrier between man and God. Our hearts, after all, are in danger of being set on fire by passion and sin. When we allow them to be set on fire with holy love, the wood that feeds the fires of passion is taken away.

In the Church of the Sacred Heart at Ehingen on the Danube, there is a painting which shows St. Thomas placing his finger in the side of Jesus. The inscription reads: *Ex tactu accepit ignem*, that is, "He touched and was set on fire." We too are set on fire when we touch the Eucharistic Lord with faith, hope, and love.

As a Communion verse in the Mass of St. Ignatius Loyola, founder of the Jesuit Order, the Church uses the words: "I have come to bring fire to the earth. How I wish it were already blazing!" Ignatius, the man of fire, was inflamed by the fire Jesus brought to earth. He passed that same fire on to his Order, and through it to the Church.

In the history of the Church there have been many saints who, like Ignatius, had hearts on fire with love. Portraits of them would have to show them with hearts on fire, as St. Augustine is sometimes pictured.

The fire Jesus brought to the earth will burn to the end of time. And wherever men are found who will allow it, that fire will communicate itself to them.

THE HOPE OF THE DYING

St. John Damascene, a Father of the Church, said with regard to Mary's death: "I will not call your holy leave-taking a dying but a falling asleep or a departing, or better, an arrival, since you are abandoning bodily life in order to reach a better life." What this Father of the Church says of Mary, we may say of all our dear dead.

Their leave-taking is not a dying but a falling asleep, a departing, an arriving. It is a falling asleep after a life that lasts a few decades, a life filled with much toil, with cares and trials, a life that often resembles a laborious journey or a hot day of heavy work. The last stretch of this journey, the final hours of this long day are usually the most difficult for the dying, but for some they are the most beautiful. The weeks of sickness bring out the hidden beauty in their souls, a beauty that throughout a lifetime had been imprisoned in the shell of human nature with its burdens; now it emerges to mark their features at the end. The face of the dying is often their truest face and tells us more about them than we had ever seen before, more than we can put into words.

Not death but a falling asleep and a departing. It is a departure from the world and from the people who have accompanied us on our journey. The departure is also painful for us who are left behind, because a human being who had been at our side as one of us is no longer there, and we feel we have become poorer and more lonely. But for the dying the departure means a liberation from the prison of human nature and this world, and the entry into a new community made up of our departed friends and forebears. But it is also an entry into a new communion with those who are left behind on earth, for death does not simply divide but also unites. Everything that had divided us, everything that stood between us, is now gone, and we have access to the real person of the other.

That is why we say "not death but a falling asleep and a departing, or better, an arrival." It is the arrival at a long-desired destination, an arrival in our homeland after a long journeying in this vale of tears, arrival in the presence of the Father, who throws his arms around us and invites us to his table. It is an arrival in the presence of Jesus, who had said: "Come to me, all you who are weary and find life burdensome, and I will refresh you" (Matthew 11:28). It is an arrival in the presence of him of whom it was said: "He was well aware of what was in man's heart" (John 2:25), that is, he knows us better than human beings know each other. It is an arrival in the presence of him of whom St. Paul says: "He will give a new form to this lowly body of ours and remake it according to the pattern of his glorified body" (Phil. 3:21).

When Jesus was departing from his disciples, his thoughts were of his coming to the Father: "If you truly loved me you would rejoice to have me go to the Father" (John 14:28). Our dear dead have also gone from us to the Father, or at least they are on their way to him. It is a source of joy to us that they have put so much of the journey behind them or may even have already reached the Father and that homeland of light, peace, and joy. They are now on the other bank of the river and beyond our sight. Yet we still seem to hear them calling to us: "Travel the way that leads to the Father so that when you die you may enter his presence! The way to the Father is Jesus. Be united to him in the Holy Eucharist, for whoever feeds on his flesh and drinks his blood possesses everlasting life. Travel with him along the way of obedience, trust, and love for the Father! Whoever has the spirit of Christ will be received by the Father."

Our dear dead also tell us: "Do not forget us! It is a fine thing to decorate our graves, but do not let your love stop there. Stay united to us and help us until we have taken the last step toward God. We expect your help, for we have earned it, and we will be grateful for it."

Archeologists uncovering the old tombs of the kings of Ur of the Chaldees have made a gruesome discovery. In the chambers of the tombs whole teams of animals have been uncovered, the skeletons still in harness. Each of the great wagons they pulled is full of artistically designed household goods, golden goblets, wonderfully shaped vases, bronze tableware, rings, harps, etc. Evidently, too, the whole household of the distinguished dead person had accompanied him. It seems that they had gone with the ox-drawn treasure wagons of the dead man into the tomb, and while the tomb was being walled up from otuside, they laid their lord to his last rest inside. Then they took poison, gathered around the dead man for the last time, and freely gave their life so that they might go on serving him in another existence.

Even more than the Chaldeans of old, we should be close to our dear ones in death and eternity. We can obtain this closeness through Jesus, our brother, who is our link with them. He brings them the prayers and good works we do in union with him and applies to them the reparation we do.

More than the Chaldeans of old, we should be sending treasures into eternity after our dear ones, treasures far more valuable than the treasures amassed by the old pagans. The treasures we can give are those we draw from the Church's treasury.

The most precious of all these treasures is the fruit of Jesus' Passion, which we send after our dear dead when we celebrate the holy sacrifice of the Mass. St. Monica asked her son St. Augustine to send that treasure after her, when she said to him before her death: "Bury my body wherever you wish; I ask only one thing of you, that you remember me at the altar of the Lord."

THE COMPASSIONATE ONE

Loneliness has become the lot of many men, and not a few can justly complain today: "No one has compassion on me." To them we must say: "There is one person who surely has compassion on you — God." Of this we have been sure ever since the Son of God became a man.

After the fall, God, knowing his holiness insulted and his love rejected, could well have left men to their fate. He could have let them travel their chosen way to its bitter end in nothingness; but he did not do so because he had compassion on us. He drove man from the garden of delights but not from his loving heart. He did not lose sight of man, and the history of salvation shows God pursuing man as a father pursues his lost son, searches him out, and brings him home.

Then the appointed time came, and God wanted to send man a redeemer. That redeemer would not be a man or an angel; it would be the Son, the Most High, for he alone could redeem men. The Son offered himself to the Father, for the love which is the Holy Spirit impelled him to do so. But the Father showed him (if we may describe things in only too human terms) that men would not welcome him but would persecute and finally crucify him. Nevertheless, the Son saw the distress of mankind and said to his Father: "Send me as mediator!" The Father agreed, and the Word became flesh. The Word had compassion on us. In him the kindness and love of God our Savior manifested itself to us.

For thirty-three years Jesus walked among us, preached the good news to us, cured the sick, and welcomed the sinners and the distressed. He called men to himself with the words. "Come to me, all you who are weary and find life burdensome, and I will refresh you" (Matthew 11:28). "He went about doing good works" (Acts 10:38), in order to show us his great kindness. But the very men he loved so deeply returned him evil for good. Some of his own people demanded that Pilate condemn him to death, and Pilate handed him over to the Jews so that they might crucify him.

According to a Spanish legend, Jesus shrank back when the soldiers brought the wood of the cross for him to carry to Calvary. But then he looked at the people standing around and thought also of the Pharisees, the executioners, and all the countless people who dwelt and dwell on earth. On them he had compassion; he wanted to give them his love.

The night in which Jesus was betrayed was the night of man's greatest ingratitude. Judas had gone to the members of the supreme council and promised to hand Jesus over to them. Jesus knew, however, that Judas' ingratitude was not unique; behind Judas he saw the long line of men who in the course of history would hate and persecute him. He foresaw all the coldness and indifference of those he would choose as his own, but he also foresaw their need. Men appeared before the eyes of his mind as sheep without a shepherd, as children with no bread to eat, as sick people without a doctor. For them his heart was full of compassion; he wanted to pour out his love on them, and since he loved us completely, he wanted to stay with us forever. Therefore, "taking bread and giving thanks, he broke it and gave it to them, saying: 'This is my body to be given for you. Do this as a remembrance of me.' He did the same with the cup after eating, saying as he did so: 'This cup is the new covenant in my blood, which will be shed for you'" (Luke 22:19-20).

Jesus has compassion on us and will continue to be compassionate throughout eternity. He will never let us slip from his loving embrace, never dismiss us into the nothingness from which we came. He will never pass us by unheedingly, never forget us. Each of us must say: "He has compassion on me. It was for me that he became a man, for me that he died on the Cross, for me that he instituted the Holy Eucharist." How consoling to know that he loves me in a wholly personal way, loves me as I am! I can tell him everything, bring him all my complaints. For this I must be grateful, and my best thanks is to give him my heart. We sing, do we not, in one of the Christmas hymns: "I give you my heart and all that I am"? And one of the poets promises us: "Give him your heart, and his heart will be yours forever" (Novalis).

If God our Father and his Son, our Redeemer, have compassion on us, then we ought to have compassion on one another. Frequently, and only too easily, we run the risk of lacking compassion, for bad experiences, disappointments, personal suffering can make our hearts narrow and hard. We must not succumb to this danger, but be constantly learning from Jesus how to have compassion for one another and to show kindness to one another. A friendly face, a sympathetic word, a helpful action are all a source of happiness for both receiver and giver. When you give your heart to others, you give them a home, you stir them to new life, and frequently you show them the way to God; in fact, you make God visible to them.

Our fellow human beings have as much, or even more, need of our heartfelt love than of our external gifts.

"Life is made up of opportunities for meeting Christ" (Guardini). Ever since Jesus became a poor helpless child at Bethlehem, he encounters us especially in those of our fellows who are poor, lonely, abandoned, misunderstood, sorrowful, and suffering. In them, he asks us: "Give me your heart!" Perhaps he lives with you, in this shape, in a room of your own house. "Accept one another, then, as Christ accepted you, for the glory of God" (Rom. 15:7), and give Christ, in others, a love that prays and blesses, forgives and renders happy.

Those who have given their hearts to Jesus have given them to their brothers and sisters as well. We need only recall Mary, the mother of fair love, St. Martin, St. Francis of Assisi, St. Elizabeth of Thueringen, or the countless martyrs of our own times. They should be our models. One Good Friday, St. John Gualbert met his brother's murderer. He wanted revenge and was ready to kill the man, when he suddenly remembered the love of the crucified Christ, forgave the murderer, and gave him the place his own brother had once had. Thus he gave his heart to a fellow human being in gratitude to Jesus, who gave us his forgiving heart.

In hell none of the damned have compassion on the others. In heaven each of the blessed opens his heart to all the others. Those who on earth have compassion for one another make life here a foretaste of heaven.

MARY AND THE SACRED HEART OF JESUS

The heart of Jesus was formed by the Holy Spirit in the womb of the Virgin Mother. Inevitably, then, Mary was closer than anyone else to the heart of Jesus both physically and spiritually. She stood by the Cross and suffered the pain of seeing a soldier pierce that heart. This piercing of Jesus' side was not part of the redemptive work which ended when Jesus said: "Now it is finished" (John 19:30), or, in Luke's report: "Father, into your hands I commend my spirit" (Luke 23:46). Nor did the soldier have special orders to pierce the side of Jesus; there was no need of it. Yet God willed that his Son's heart be pierced by the soldier's spear. Why? He wanted to show us that the heart, that is, the love, of Jesus is the source of redemption and that it is from this heart that the streams of forgiveness and grace flow out over the world.

Mary was close at hand when Jesus' heart was pierced, and she began to have some inkling of why this mysterious event took place. She grasped it fully, however, only when the Holy Spirit was poured out upon the Church at Pentecost, for the Holy Spirit taught her to enter more deeply into the mind of God and to love and venerate the mystery God was manifesting in the piercing of Jesus' heart. In this way Mary became the supreme example of veneration of the Sacred Heart and the model of Sacred Heart devotion for the Church as a whole.

1. *We venerate the heart of Jesus by our trust.*

Jesus bids us trust in him when he says: "Come to me, all you who are weary and find life burdensome, and I will

141

refresh you. . . . Your souls will find rest" (Matthew 11: 28-29). In Jesus the kindness of our God and his love for men have found visible expression, for the heart of Jesus too is full of kindness and love; it is a treasury of blessings for all who call upon him. The opened side of Jesus is like an open door, a flowing spring, a throne of grace. His heart is a refuge and place of rest for all men, and everyone — children, the poor, the sick, the scorned, the dying — has access to it. "My heart is moved with pity for the crowd," Jesus said just before he multiplied the loaves and gave the crowd more food than it could eat (Matthew 15:32). His heart is both kind and powerful.

Mary knew this, for she knew Jesus better than anyone else did. That is why she immediately put in a good word for the newly married couple at Cana and told the Lord: "They have no more wine" (John 2:3). Jesus had as yet worked no public miracle, but Mary knew both the power and the overflowing kindness of her Son. She knew he would not fail to answer her plea and would hasten the appointed hour for his work to begin.

We, like Mary, should have unlimited trust in the Lord. The heart of Jesus feels both joy and honor when we come to him with important needs. But the thing we ought to pray for most of all is the spirit of the Sacred Heart of Jesus. That spirit is the most important thing we can ask for and the most valuable thing Jesus can give us. He will give that good spirit to those who ask for it. The spirit of the heart of Jesus is the spirit of reparation.

2. *We venerate the heart of Jesus by making reparation.*

Reparation captures the deepest meaning of the Sacred Heart devotion. "Reparation" means making up for harm done, retrieving what has been lost. Concretely, reparation means making satisfaction first for our own sins, then for the sins of others. The intention of making reparation causes the soul not simply to repent of the evil done but to make up for it, to cleanse the world of it, as it were. It seeks to retrieve what was lost through sin. The person who has the spirit of reparation considers, moreover, that the sins of which others do not repent are, as it were, an injustice to him personally.

Jesus, of course, became a sacrifice of reparation for all the sinners of the world, offering himself on the Cross to the Father in order to make up for all sins. The reparation he offered with a loving heart was superabundant, infinitely outweighing all sin. Can we imagine anyone with a scales big enough to measure the value of what Jesus did?

Mary stood beside the Cross. The suffering of Jesus brought home to her the extent and gravity of sin, but the loving self-sacrifice of her Son also enabled her to glimpse the infinite reparation which could offset all sins, however numerous.

Mary also shared in her Son's work of reparation, making up, as it were, what was still lacking in the reparation offered by Jesus Christ, insofar as the members of the Mystical Body are called to cooperate with the reparative sacrifice of their Head.

When Jesus on the Cross asked his Father to forgive men, Mary prayed with him. When he offered his life in reparation with the words, "Father, into your hands I commend my spirit" (Luke 23:46), she uttered the same prayer in her heart. When Jesus offered sacrifice, Mary offered with him. She presented her Son's reparation with her own hands to his Father, as it were, and united her own love and obedience to the reparative love and reparative obedience of Jesus. Her sacrifice could not but reach God and be pleasing to him.

We too must offer reparation to God. But our human

reparation would by itself be worthless in his eyes. The only reparation we can truly offer God is the one Mary offered, the reparation of her Son. Our acts of reparation — prayer, penance, suffering, work, sacrifice, acts of love — however insignificant they may seem, acquire value in God's sight and are acceptable to him when they are placed in the heart of Jesus and become part of his reparative activity — in other words, when they are laid on the altar of sacrifice which is the heart of Jesus and are offered through the loving hands of God's mother.

The brothers of Joseph, who had been carried off to Egypt, showed Jacob, their father, the blood-stained garments of their brother and thus brought him great pain and sorrow. We show God, our Father, the heart of his Son that has been wounded by our sins and thus bring him consolation as well as reparation for our sins.

Isaac smelled the odor of his elder son's garments and blessed Jacob, who had clad himself in them. In a similar way, God is pleased when we unite our own reparation to that of his Son; he accepts it and blesses us. We can best unite ourselves to Jesus in this way at the celebration of holy Mass.

Mary offered reparation not only to God the Father but also to the Savior. He suffered greatly from the mockery of the people, the blasphemies of the chief priests and members of the supreme council, and the flight of his disciples. But he also found immense consolation in Mary as she stood beside the Cross. Courageously, faithfully, perseveringly she was professing her faith in him and thus sharing his suffering and taking it on herself. She did not hesitate to remain there as his mother. We should thank Mary for offering reparation to the Savior in this way. There, at the Cross, she, along with John and a few devoted women, represented Mother Church, who will, to the end of time, offer reparation to the heart of Jesus for the sins of her own children and those of all mankind.

The prayer of the contemplative Orders, the devotional exercises of the faithful, the celebration of the Church's liturgy, the reception of the sacraments of penance and the Holy Eucharist, and the suffering of the faithful who consecrate their lives to Christ are all valuable forms of reparation to the Sacred Heart.

On one occasion Jesus showed his heart to St. Margaret Mary Alacoque and complained: "See this heart, which so loves men that it exhausts and spends itself to prove its love to them. Yet, in reward I receive from most men only ingratitude in the form of irreverence and blasphemy, coldness and contempt for me in the sacrament of love. But it is even more painful for me to see hearts consecrated to me acting in the same way" (Jesus to Margaret Mary Alacoque during the octave of Corpus Christi, 1675). Then the Lord asked for a special feast of reparation and promised the fullness of his love to those who would make up to him for the honor denied him by others.

Who can reject the wish of this heart so on fire with love? Who can fail to respond with love to so loving a Lord? Even if he had not given us his great promises, we ought never rest from making acts of reparation to him throughout our lives. "The urge to make reparation must be awakened and strengthened wherever souls are lovers of God and friends of Christ" (Prohaska).

The reparation we offer in our own day already gave consolation to the Lord during his Passion, since before God past, present, and future are all present. Repentant, grateful, loving meditation on the life, suffering, and death of Jesus is already an act of reparation. Our actions and labors, the fulfillment of our daily duties, indeed our whole lives insofar as we put them under obedience to God's will can be offered to Jesus as a sacrifice of reparation. We need only say: "Most Sacred Heart of Jesus, in reparation I consecrate myself to you through Mary!"

THE BEGINNING AND THE END

During the blessing of the paschal candle the priest scratches a cross on the candle. Then, above the upright beam of the cross, he draws the Greek letter for *a* (alpha) and, under it, the Greek letter for *ō* (omega). As he does so he says:

Christ yesterday and today,
the beginning and the end,
Alpha and Omega;
all time belongs to him,
and all the ages:
to him be glory and power,
through every age for ever. Amen.

Man spends each day amid the turning wheels and each night sees the flashing billboards; he watches the events of the day pass before him on the television screen or follows the developments in world politics. He may toil and find pleasure, but he must also suffer and die. Inevitably he asks himself: "What is the point of all this? What is the world really all about? Why does it exist? Where do I come from and where am I going?"

During the Easter Vigil the Church invites the person who asks these questions to stand before the silently burning paschal candle that the priest has just blessed. Here, in front of the candle with its alpha and omega, he will find the answer to his questions.

Taking his station near the candle, which is a symbol of Christ, the lector reads of the world's beginning: "In the

beginning, when God created the heavens and the earth . . ."
(Gen. 1:1). With this first reading the Church seeks to
make the faithful vividly aware that the world has its origin
in God, its beginning in him who is symbolized by the
paschal candle. He says of himself in the Apocalypse: "I am
the Alpha" (Rev. 21:6). St. John expresses the very same
thought at the beginning of his Gospel: "In the beginning
was the Word, and the Word was with God; and the Word
was God. He was in the beginning with God. All things were
made through him, and without him was not anything made
that was made" (John 1:1-3RSV).

Before heaven and earth came into existence and
before time began to run, God thought an all-embracing
thought that expressed his whole being. This thought was
the eternal Word, Christ in his pre-temporal existence.
"The Word was with God," for his origin, his home, his
dwelling place is in God, in the Father, and from the Father
he comes forth. He is the mirror in whom the Father, with an
eternal delight, sees himself and all conceivable beings.

Everything created has come into existence through
the Word. In the Word, God's eternal thought, all things
apart from God are conceived; in him the whole plan that
underlies the world, nature, grace, and glory exists. In
him everything has its eternal ground, and from him
everything comes forth. From him everything that is or was
or will be derives its content and consistency, and without his doing nothing comes into existence — not a single
atom or grain of sand or flower or animal or man. Every
being has its origin and home in him.

The world, then, has its origin and meaning from
Christ. This is why St. Paul the Apostle can write: "He is
the image of the invisible God, the first-born of all creatures. In him everything in heaven and on earth was created,
things visible and invisible. . . . all were created through him,
and for him. He is before all else that is. In him everything

continues in being. It is he who is . . . the beginning, the first-born of the dead, so that primacy may be his in everything" (Col. 1:16-18).

The world was marvelously created by Christ, and man, as he searches, is constantly discovering more of the wonders of creation. Einstein writes that the laws of nature point to an intellect so superior that all meaningful human thought and organization are but a very distant reflection of it (see Einstein, *The World as I See It*).

But into this beautifully ordered world the first human beings introduced disorder by their sin. Then Christ gave the world a new beginning, so that its new state was even more wonderful than the original. "The Word was made flesh and dwelt among us" (John 1:14KJ). He became a man within the stream of time so that he might save the world. The child who lay in the manger and received Mary's adoration is the second divine Person and, as such, older by far than the rocks of Bethlehem's cave or the stars that twinkled in the heavens during that holy night. This Person is not, like Abraham, simply one member in the long line of God's servants, for he can say of himself: "Before Abraham came to be, I AM" (John 8:58).

He came into the world to consecrate and sanctify it and make it truly God's possession. Thus, through the humanity of God's Son, the created world turned back to God once again. "It pleased God to make absolute fullness reside in him and, by means of him, to reconcile everything in his person, both on earth and in the heavens, making peace through the blood of his cross" (Col. 1:19-20). Christ completed this return of the world to God that had begun in the Incarnation by his sacrificial death on the Cross and his resurrection. He has founded a new creation that is consecrated to God and sanctified for him and that in Christ has become truly God's possession.

As the sun descends into the darkness (that was how

people in Christ's day conceived of the setting of the sun), so Christ by dying descended into night and then, in his resurrection, emerged again like the rising sun. He brought the world to a new day, the day of salvation.

"Christ brought the world out of darkness into daylight. He destroyed the lifeless darkness and spread life throughout the universe, so that the universe is now filled with the indescribable light of the Beginning. The rising sun streams through the world, and therefore we who believe live amid radiant day" (Hippolytus). Every Sunday, the first day of the new week, we celebrate the resurrection of Christ and thank the Lord for bringing the world to the new day of salvation by his resurrection from the dead. "Let your every creature serve you; for you spoke, and they were made" (Judith 16:14).

Christ is the beginning of our own existence, too. From all eternity we were part of Christ's plan and were present in his mind. With the Psalmist we can therefore say to him: "My soul also you knew full well; nor was my frame unknown to you when I was made in secret, when I was fashioned in the depths of the earth. Your eyes have seen my actions; in your book they are all written; my days were limited before one of them existed" (Ps. 139:14-16).

We were born into the world, but that birth would have been useless to us if salvation had not come through Christ's redemptive work.

During the blessing of the baptismal water at the Easter Vigil, the Church prays: "Father, look now with love upon your Church, and unseal for her the fountain of baptism. By the power of the Spirit give to the water of this font the grace of your Son. You created man in your likeness: cleanse him from sin in a new birth of innocence by water and the Spirit." In baptism we were born anew and recreated. Thus Christ gave us a second beginning, a new life that is a sharing in God's own life. Now our lives are permeated by the power of Christ, who consecrates and sanctifies us for the sake of the all-holy God and Father of all things.

Should we be so unfortunate as to lose this life, the Lord in his love will begin anew with us if we turn back to him with repentance and a firm purpose of amendment in the sacrament of penance, which has been called a "second baptism." The Lord in his love and mercy will always begin again with us.

We should adore the Lord as the source of our being and thank him for giving us the possibility of beginning ever anew in him. We should not let this possibility be fruitless. Christ is the Beginning that has no beginning, and the End that has no end. He is both Beginning and End together.

* * *

At the end of time all men will see what it was given John to see on Patmos.

> Then I saw new heavens and a new earth. The former heavens and the former earth had passed away, and the sea was no longer. I also saw a new Jerusalem, the holy city, coming down out of heaven from God, beautiful as a bride prepared to meet her husband. I heard a loud voice from the throne cry out: "This is God's dwelling among men. He shall dwell with them and they shall be his people and he shall be their God who is always with them. He shall wipe every tear from their eyes, and there shall be no more death or mourning, crying out or pain, for the former world has passed away." The One who sat on the throne said to me, "See, I make all things new!" Then he said, "Write these matters down, for the words are trustworthy and true!" He went on to say: "These words are already fulfilled! I am the Alpha and the Omega, the Beginning and the End" (Rev. 21:1-6).

Jesus is the Omega, the End and Fulfillment of creation. He will liberate the world from all the evil and disorder that have entered it through sin, and will fill it with unending glory. Thus creation will, after its own fashion, share in the resurrection of the body. Jesus is also the Omega, the End and Fulfillment of man. At the end he will bring fulfillment to those who have believed in him, hoped in him, and loved him. From this inner core of faith, hope, and love he will reshape the whole of the believer's life through all that he has done and suffered, and will bring it to its eternally perfect form.

Jesus is the Omega, because he is the *Son of God*.

Through the Incarnation man's entire being was taken up into the person of the Logos, and is elevated, supported, permeated, and sanctified by His divine person. In the absolutely eternal person of the Son of God the body He assumed necessarily receives a call and a claim to everlasting existence. The same call and claim are received by the bodies of all the living members that have been mediately incorporated into the God-man's own body. The fact that the eternal God has entered into perishable flesh and has taken that flesh up with Him to the bosom of the eternal God, is the final and supreme reason for its everlasting duration and its triumphant victory over death (Scheeben, *The Mysteries of Christianity*, pp. 670–71).

In the Incarnate Son, God's concern for man has reached its climactic expression, for in Christ, God and mankind have not only touched but have become one. In Christ, mankind's goal has been achieved and its true future has begun. God is now at home in this world of ours. "Mankind can advance no further or higher than it has, for God is the furthest and the highest. . . . God's final decision for man has already been made" (Joseph Ratzinger, *Introduction to Christianity*, p. 199).

Christ is the Omega because *he has redeemed the world* by his suffering and death. "He emptied himself and took the form of a slave. . . . He humbled himself, obediently accepting even death, death on a cross!" (Phil. 2:7-8). He made himself the crowning member of creation, just as Omega is the final letter of the Greek alphabet. And yet he could say of himself: "I am a worm, not a man; the scorn of men, despised by the people" (Ps. 22:7).

By his love, which is stronger than death, he broke the bonds of death and the barrier it had set up for men, and opened a definitive future for man and the world. God it was who gave him the victory. "God highly exalted him and bestowed on him the name above every other name, so that at Jesus' name every knee must bend in the heavens, on the earth, and under the earth, and every tongue proclaim to the glory of God the Father: JESUS CHRIST IS LORD!" (Phil. 2:9-11).

At the Second Vatican Council, the Church spoke as follows of Christ, the Alpha and the Omega:

> The Lord is the goal of human history, the focal point of the desires of history and civilization, the center of mankind, the joy of all hearts, and the fulfillment of all aspirations. It is he whom the Father raised from the dead, exalted and placed at his right hand, constituting him judge of the living and the dead. Animated and drawn together in his Spirit we press onwards on our journey towards the consummation of history which fully corresponds to the plan of his love: "to unite all things in him, things in heaven and things on earth" (*Pastoral Constitution on the Church in the Modern World*, no. 45).

God thus made his Son, Jesus Christ, the Omega, the center and Lord of the world. Whoever accepts him by faith finds the fulfillment of his longing for salvation and experiences the breakthrough of the rule of God in him.

But many do not believe in him. "He came unto his own, and his own received him not" (John 1:11KJ). The message of the Cross was "a stumbling block to Jews, and an absurdity to Gentiles" (1 Cor. 1:23). Many persons of that day were running after false prophets, and many today believe in Marx or Mao rather than in Christ. The Lord foresaw this phenomenon and predicted the coming of false prophets, especially in the final period: "If anyone tells you at that time, 'Look, the Messiah is here,' or 'He is there,' do not believe it. False messiahs and false prophets will appear, performing signs and wonders so great as to mislead even the chosen if that were possible" (Matthew 24: 23-24).

In the final period promises of salvation will come from every likely or unlikely quarter. Then the believing Christian must hold fast to Christ, even though an angel from heaven were to come and preach a different gospel. There will be hours of testing for Christians of the final period, just as there were for John the Baptist. "John in prison heard about the works Christ was performing, and sent a message by his disciples to ask him, 'Are you "He who is to come" or do we look for another?' In reply, Jesus said to them: 'Go back and report to John what you hear and see: the blind recover their sight, cripples walk, lepers are cured, the deaf hear, dead men are raised to life, and the poor have the good news preached to them'" (Matthew 11:2-5). John thus points to the testimony of his miracles as showing him to be the Messiah foretold by the prophet Isaias. What the prophets anticipated has come to pass in him.

The miracles of Jesus proved his divinity, "for no man can perform signs and wonders such as you perform unless God is with him" (John 3:2). Man is made for God and can find fulfillment only through union with God. Such a union is in turn possible for us only in Christ. Our union began in him and must be completed in him, for now that God has become a man in the person of Christ, it is only in and through Christ that the rest of men can have access to God. If a man tries to reach God apart from Christ, he fails completely. Christ is the man who had his existence in God and through whom God entered human life. Jesus put this truth in these words: "No one comes to the Father but through me" (John 14:6), and "Whoever has seen me has seen the Father" (John 14:9).

Because Christ is our only way to the Father and thus to our own fulfillment, we no longer need ask him: "Are you 'He who is to come' or do we look for another?" Rather, we confess to him, who alone can be our goal: "You are the Messiah, the Son of the living God!" (Matthew 16:16). "Lord, to whom shall we go? You have the words of eternal life. We have come to believe; we are convinced that you are God's holy one" (John 6:68-69).

It was through faith that Peter came to know Jesus. So too it is only through faith, to begin with, that we can know Christ to be our goal. But at the end of time faith will give way to vision.

At the beginning of his Gospel John directs our attention to him who was "in the beginning." In the Apocalypse, the last book of Sacred Scripture, he directs our attention to him who will be at the end and to whom we are to hasten with the glad cry: "*Maran atha*! — Come, Lord Jesus!" We must cling to our glorious hope until the end (cf. Heb. 3:6), like "those servants whom the master finds wide-awake on his return" (Luke 12:37).

THE GOOD SHEPHERD

Jesus, the eternal Shepherd, came to earth looking for the lost sheep. It was in a town of shepherds that he appeared in our world, and his first home was a stable, where the flocks took shelter at night. Moreover, pious shepherds were the first to adore the eternal Shepherd in the manger.

When, after thirty years of hidden existence, he finally came forth among men to gather his flock, he told them: "I am the good shepherd; the good shepherd lays down his life for the sheep. . . . I know my sheep and my sheep know me in the same way that the Father knows me and I know the Father" (John 10:11, 14-15).

The parable of the Good Shepherd is one of the most attractive in the whole of Scripture, just as the title "Good Shepherd" is one of the most beautiful Jesus took for himself. Images of Jesus as the Good Shepherd were and are among the favorite pictures of Christians. They adorn the catacombs in Rome, and are to be found on confessionals and apses. One of the most beautiful of them is to be found in Ravenna. We may say that the image of the Good Shepherd was the earlier version of the picture of the Sacred Heart.

The good shepherd knows his sheep. He knows each individual with its strengths and weaknesses, for he has his eye on each. He is always with his sheep, not leaving them even at night, for he sleeps in his shepherd's hut so as to be on the spot if thieves or wolves should threaten the flock. Other animals have inborn ways of hiding themselves or weapons for defending themselves. The sheep has neither. It is weak, helpless, defenseless; it easily goes astray and is subject to many diseases. For this reason it depends on the shepherd's protection. The shepherd is its defender and source of strength.

Jesus is our shepherd and knows us as his Father knows him. He knows our good and bad points, but his knowledge is the knowledge of one who loves and always finds reason to excuse us, as he did the Jewish people from the Cross: "Father, forgive them; they do not know what they are doing" (Luke 23:34).

He is always with me (cf. Ps. 23:4). The tabernacle of the little mission chapel no less than of the great cathedral, the domestic chapel of the hospital or seminary — these are his shepherd's hut, and here he is present. From his hut he gazes out at the person who prays there, presenting his need, telling his love, or offering thanks for joys received. To the Lord in the tabernacle we can say: "I shall not want. . . . for you are at my side with your rod and your staff that give me courage" (Ps. 23:1,4). "He neither slumbers nor sleeps, the guardian of Israel" (Ps. 121:4).

A shepherd is never idle, but always concerned for his flock. In the early morning he opens the gate of the sheepfold. The sheep recognize him, run to meet him, and leap up at him, as though they wanted to show their joy at his coming. So too we should rejoice when the Lord meets us. For like a shepherd he comes to console us and lead us to good pasture. He wants to lead us out to green pastures and refresh us beside restful waters. The pasture to which this Good Shepherd leads us is the Holy Eucharist that he has planted in order to nourish his sheep, and has watered with his blood. A wonderful pasture is this, a meadow far greater than all other meadows; its food never loses its freshness, and its sweetness never leads to distaste or satiety.

The shepherd leads his flock to pasture; he goes before,

and they follow him. He passes by a green field of clover, for though the sheep would like to pasture there, he holds them back, knowing that the clover would only bloat them. He passes by a pool of water, for though the sheep would like to run to it and drink, he knows the water is unhealthy. Down in the valley lies thick grass, but the shepherd does not lead his flock to it, for he knows the grass is bitter and will make the sheep sick.

Jesus, the Good Shepherd, often keeps us from something we think good, and we are tempted to think that he wants us to have no joy in life. In reality, however, he only seeks to keep evil from us. His interest is in the well-being of the sheep, not their wool from which he might profit. We ought to fear no evil from his protecting hand; we should listen to his voice and not the alluring voice of the seducer.

Not all sheep follow a good shepherd. One or the other rejects his protecting care and goes off to seek fodder of its own. But once away from the flock, it becomes unsure of itself and soon cannot find the path. Fear only drives it further into danger, as it goes astray in the thickets and wanders by untrodden paths amid the boulders into the forest. It climbs dangerous cliffs; every sound frightens it anew and makes it hurry on. When a sheep no longer hears the voice of its kindly shepherd, it feels terror at the rustling of the branches, the roaring of the wind, and the movement of a pebble.

Such is the picture of someone who has abandoned Jesus, the Good Shepherd. He can no longer say: "I fear no evil; for you are at my side with your rod and your staff that give me courage" (Ps. 23:4). He has lost his place in the Shepherd's arms, no longer feels the Shepherd's eye on him, the Shepherd's protecting arms about him, the Shepherd's voice guiding him. Fear is the fodder of the man who has abandoned Jesus.

A good shepherd does not dismiss the straying sheep

from his thoughts. He goes after the sheep over hill and dale, through storm and rain, wounding his feet and bloodying his hands. He looks for the sheep's tracks and tries to judge whether a piece of wool in a thornbush marks the passage of his sheep. The good shepherd does not give up the pursuit but leaves the ninety-nine behind and concentrates on the one that is lost. He seeks it as though he loved this one sheep alone. The hireling, who does not own the sheep, would long since have forgotten the stray, for he has no interest either in the value of the sheep or in the property of its owner.

Finally, the good shepherd discovers the sheep. It stands immobilized by fear atop a steep crag. The eagle is circling above it, waiting to take it to its eyrie; the wolf is prowling down below, waiting to tear it to pieces. If the sheep were to take a single step, it would plunge down the precipice and become a prey to the wolf. The shepherd immediately sees the sheep's danger and knows he must not frighten it. Calling on his last reserves of strength, he climbs the crag on bloody feet and with pounding heart. Once on top, he avoids everything that might send the sheep plunging to destruction. He does not curse it or strike it or drive it before him, but calls it gently to him, takes it in his arms, puts it on his shoulder, and carries it home. With one hand he clasps the sheep to himself, with the other he wards off the attack of the eagle and wolf. Once home, he lets the sheep join the rest of the flock. How happy he is that he has found his sheep! His joy cannot contain itself, and he tells his friends: "Rejoice with me because I have found my lost sheep" (Luke 15:6).

As a good shepherd seeks his lost sheep, so Jesus, the Good Shepherd, seeks us. He chose to become himself a Lamb and to let himself be trodden underfoot by the rebellious flock so that he might, at the price of his life, regain both flock and pasture. For us he climbed the hill of Calvary. Even now he pursues us, seeking to draw us from the thornbush of sin through the sacrament of penance. He brings us together as his united flock. As sheep gather in groups for greater safety in danger or for protection against the midday heat, so we must gather into a community under the leadership of the Good Shepherd so as to find security and protection. In the community which is the Church, Jesus is the Good Shepherd, and he seeks to make us part of that community. All men are in fact his sheep, because he died for them all. He wants to bring them all together; they are to hear his voice so that there may be but one flock and one shepherd (cf. John 10:16).

Even if we should walk in the valley of death, we need fear no evil because the Shepherd is with us. So that we may lack for nothing, he provides us with a special sacrament for the hour of death. In it he anoints the members of the dying sheep with oil, cleanses the soul from any sins still on it, consoles it against the fear of death, and in the last hour helps it say a willing yes to God, thus turning death into an act of adoration. Blessed is he who dies in the loving arms of the Good Shepherd and in his pastures of grace!

When the person has passed through death and has long since been nourishing his soul in the meadows of heaven, the Day comes on which the eternal Shepherd musters the whole vast flock that he created and redeemed. With his staff he then separates the sheep from the goats. The latter he drives away forever, but the blessed sheep he and the singing angels lead into the sheepfold of eternal blessedness and the eternal pasture which he himself is (cf. Rev. 7: 15-17).

Thank your Shepherd for his love! Listen to his

voice and follow him! Gaze trustingly into his eyes and do not make his burden as Shepherd any heavier! Help him in his work, and through your word, example, and prayer lead other souls to him! Take no sheep away from him by giving scandal, for then, in his eyes, you would be playing the part of the wolf and the thief!

THE ONE WHOSE "LOVE NEVER FAILS" (1 COR. 13:8)

People today are unwilling to commit themselves unreservedly to anything. Even Catholics shy away from a definitive disposition of their lives and prefer to talk of temporary marriage, temporary priests, temporary vows, and even temporary Christianity. They want to be Catholics for as long as it pleases them, to be "good" with numerous, very numerous, reservations. Others want to be Catholic to the extent only of doing what they must under pain of sin but nothing more.

If the Savior were to ask them, as he asked his disciples in the synagogue at Capernaum: "Do you want to leave me too?" (John 6:67), many might well answer: "We would like to give you a try, but we can't commit ourselves definitively." They would like to postpone any hour of decision determined by Jesus and substitute for it an hour which it is for them to determine.

Anyone with this attitude is putting the axe to the very roots of life in Christ. He questions the basic attitude of the Christian, which is the wholehearted love St. Paul speaks of: "Love never fails" (1 Cor. 13:8). God's love, revealed and given to us in Jesus Christ, our Lord, never fails.

God gave us his love in Jesus, his Son, and his love is everlasting. "With age-old love I have loved you," he told us through his prophet (Jer. 31:3). God's love never fails, for it has no end marked by time; it is eternal; it has no beginning and no end.

The mountains may sink into the sea, the stars fall from heaven, and the world go up in flames, but God's love will never end, even though men reject it. God will never say: "I have done enough. No more!"

God's love is not limited in measure, for nothing can eradicate it from his heart. He created the world out of love and handed it over to men that it might serve them. Men refused God the obedience due him, but his love did not give up on fallen man. Instead, he redeemed the sinner and entered upon a course of action that makes his love incomprehensible to us, for he did not send an angel or a man, but his own Son to redeem the world.

God could have redeemed the world without the incarnation of his Son, or if he wanted that incarnation, it would have been perfectly adequate by itself. But even the simple incarnation was not enough for this God who loves; he wanted to do more. Sin was great, but grace should show itself greater still. God gave his Son over to death; he even chose for him the most shameful and difficult death man has ever suffered, for the greatness of the suffering would bring home to us the greatness of the love. "There is no greater love than this: to lay down one's life for one's friends" (John 15:13), said Jesus, thinking of himself.

As Jesus was carrying his Cross to Calvary, the soldiers became afraid that his strength was running out, and they forced Simon of Cyrene to help Jesus carry his burden. But Jesus' love was not running out! No, it drew on every ounce of strength that was in him, as he allowed himself to be nailed to the Cross and raised aloft on it. Suffering terribly, he hung there on the wood of shame, with the Jews mocking him and calling out to him: "He saved others but he cannot save himself! Let the 'Messiah,' the 'king of Israel,' come down from that cross" (Mark 15:31-32). He indeed had the needed power to come down from the Cross, but his love, far more than the nails in hands and feet, kept him on it.

Jesus persevered to the end. Not even in his feeling of abandonment by God did he say:"I can take no more!" He did not give in until the final demand of love had been met and he could say: "Now it is finished" (John 19:30). For the love that burned in his heart was like a fire that will not go out until it has burned up all its material.

The beams of the Cross were limited in breadth and height and length and depth, but the love of Jesus was unlimited. Loving us, he loved us to the very utmost. Moreover, his limitless love was such that he wished to remain with us in the Blessed Eucharist, and so he instituted the memorial of his suffering and his love, intending to stay among us as our companion on the journey, our priest of sacrifice, and our food.

His love took on an especially affectionate tone after his resurrection. Thus we see the risen Lord gathering his scattered flock and showing them the great love of the Good Shepherd. And how lovingly he spoke to Magdalene in the garden on Easter morning, to Thomas, who recognized Jesus by this love, and to Peter, to whom he revealed himself in a special way when he was downcast by his betrayal of the Lord.

A servant can give notice that he is leaving his position, but a mother cannot give notice that her love is ended! And even if she could, the loving Lord could never do it. If he did, he would be denying his own nature. God therefore assures us through the prophet: "Can a mother forget her infant, be without tenderness for the child of her womb? Even should she forget, I will never forget you" (Is. 49:15).

God's limitless love showed itself most fully and beautifully to the Mother of the Lord, for she was the first object of his love. It was his love that chose her and poured grace out upon her. Jesus, in turn, was unwilling to die until he had provided for his mother, and it was to her that he addressed some of his final words: "Woman, behold thy son" (John 19:26KJ).

Mary loved Jesus in return with a limitless love. The Holy Spirit himself had enkindled love for Jesus in her heart, and the flame was never to be extinguished. That love showed itself most clearly during the suffering of her Son. She hastened to the place of execution; she stayed by the Cross to the bitter end; she accompanied her Son's body to its tomb. Mary never said: "I can take no more!" The only words on her lips were: "I am the servant of the Lord" (Luke 1:38).

In Mary, suffering love then turned into hoping love, for her love bade her hope for her Son's resurrection. After his Ascension, her love became a love of yearning for Jesus. Now, ever since her Assumption into heaven, her love of the Lord is a love that adores and gives thanks.

Faith gives rise in us to love for God, and that love, like his love for us, must have no end or limitation of degree. As God never ceases to love us, we must never cease to love God and Jesus.

In one of the hymns, we sing: "I will love you, Light all-beautiful, until my heart is stilled in death." As we are dying, our words should be those of St. Therese of the Child Jesus: "My God, I love you!"

Our love must not be limited in degree. We must never say: "I have fulfilled my duty and done all I should. The rest I can let go. Can God ask any more of me?" Being a Christian should not mean stopping where duty ends.

"What counts is total commitment" (Sartre). In the spiritual life we must not be satisfied with small accomplishments and be "minimalists"! We must rather be generous of heart and be constantly striving to live so as to please God the more (cf. Rom. 12:2).

Halfway love feels wounds, wholehearted love brings joy. Wholehearted love makes us obey God's commandments out of love, carry the crosses God gives us, and accept his calls to imitate Christ. Anyone who has experienced how happy love for Jesus makes him will always be seeking to fill his heart with love. He will strive to offer Jesus ever greater adoration, thanksgiving, reparation, and fidelity.

As a fire does not stop burning as long as it has material to feed it, so the love of Jesus should continue to feed on us. In order to prevent the flame of love from going out, we must constantly renew our faith in God's love for us and feed our love through frequent reception of the Holy Eucharist, as well as through prayer and sacrifice.

May the Lord take us to himself in heaven so that we may be able to love him throughout eternity.

> Bless the Lord, O my soul,
>   and forget not all his benefits. . . .
> For as the heavens are high above the earth,
>   so surpassing is his kindness toward those
>   who fear him.
> As far as the east is from the west,
>   so far has he put our transgressions from us.
> As a father has compassion on his children,
>   so the Lord has compassion on those
>   who fear him,
> For he knows how we are formed;
>   he remembers that we are dust. . . .
> But the kindness of the Lord is from eternity
>   to eternity toward those who fear him,
> And his justice toward children's children
>   among those who keep his covenant
>   and remember to fulfill his precepts.
>   (Ps. 103:2, 11-14, 17-18)

O mystery of mysteries, that the ineffable love of Father to Son should be the love of the Son to us!

Why was it, O Lord? What good thing didst Thou see in me a sinner? Why wast Thou set on me? "What is man, that Thou art mindful of him, and the son of man that Thou visitest him?" This poor flesh of mine, this weak sinful soul, which has no life except in Thy grace, Thou didst set Thy love upon it. Complete Thy work, O Lord, and as Thou hast loved me from the beginning, so make me love Thee unto the end (John Henry Cardinal Newman).

Jesus, I believe in you until the time of vision comes;
I hope in you, until I reach my home with you.
I love you till I see your face,
and seeing, I shall love eternally (Johann M. Sailer).

THE CORNERSTONE

King Nabuchodonosor once had a dream in which he saw a large, shining statue with a face that struck terror into him. Its head was of pure gold, its chest and arms of silver, its belly and thighs of bronze, its legs of iron, and its feet partly of iron, partly of tile. Then, without any human intervention, a stone hewn from a mountain struck the iron and tile feet and broke them to pieces. In a moment, iron, tile, bronze, silver, and gold all crumbled and were blown away by the wind. The stone, however, grew into a great mountain and filled the earth (cf. Dan. 2).

The stone that left the mountain without any human intervention is Jesus. He came from his heavenly Father, freely following his own eternal plan and without dependence on any human being. As he came from the Father without human intervention, so he took up his dwelling in Mary's womb without human intervention, solely by the power of the Spirit. The stone was as small as a man's fist, and yet it shattered the mighty statue.

Jesus came upon the scene of this world as a helpless child, and yet what a shattering effect he had! He laid hold of the world and effected a transformation, a radical change in the history of mankind. Christ's coming was an event that turned everything upside down. The change is still going on, because Jesus still comes to transform the world, even though men may not see this or want to see it.

The stone that fell from the mountain in an apparently accidental way, far away from us on a distant peak, came closer to us. It grew and grew and is still growing today into a great mountain and filling the earth. Jesus is the stone that grows into a mountain and fills the earth; he is the holy mountain on which the hand of the Lord rests (Is. 25:10) and which the Lord blesses, the mountain to which men look with confidence and to which they make their pilgrimage.

Christ, the stone that became a mountain, covers the whole earth. Nothing escapes his influence. In Jesus Christ all things have, after all, been created. To Jesus Christ all power in heaven and on earth has been given, and all things owe him their continued existence.

In the Gospel Jesus speaks of his Father who makes the sun rise on the good and the bad, and sends rain upon the just and the unjust, whether or not they thank him for it. In a similar way, Jesus can fulfill his role as cornerstone, whether or not we know of it. All that is good in this world and in the souls of men is there because of the active presence of Jesus, even though that presence may not be recognized.

Jesus is the mountain, and we must not simply build on that mountain or look to it, but we must climb it. The ascent is steep, as though the mountain were the Mount of Olives or the Hill of Calvary. The climb takes great effort, for the Lord tells us: "If a man wishes to come after me, he must deny his very self, take up his cross, and begin to follow in my footsteps" (Matthew 16:24). "Where I am, there will my servant be" (John 12:26). To follow Christ means to become like him, to take on his features, to try in a small way to be what he is, and to pattern oneself after him.

The image of the mountain also reminds us of the rock from which Moses drew water with a blow of his staff. Jesus is the rock from which the water of grace and mercy flows out upon the whole world.

Jesus is not only the stone that becomes a world-filling mountain; he is also the foundation stone or cornerstone on which every spiritual building must be erected.

On one occasion, as he gazed at the mighty blocks of which the Temple was built, Jesus reminded his hearers of what the Psalmist had said: "The stone which the builders rejected has become the cornerstone" (Ps. 118:22; cf. Matthew 21:42). He was referring the text to himself and saying that he was not simply *a* cornerstone but *the* cornerstone. The holy Apostle Paul speaks of Christ as being the foundation of the building which is the Church (1 Cor. 3:11). He is also the foundation of the Christian's life.

Our Christian life rests upon Jesus, the cornerstone; however, this dependence is by no means the same as that experienced by the followers of important historical figures such as Plato, Goethe, Hegel, Kant, Karl Marx, Teilhard de Chardin, etc.

Our Christian existence has its foundation in Jesus because, being the incarnate *Son of God*, he is the living and life-giving presence of God to us and is consequently our beginning, our life, our strength, and our goal. Our Christian existence rests on him also because he cleansed us with his blood and "made us a royal nation of priests in the service of his God and Father" (Rev. 1:6).

He made our kind of existence his own, while setting aside all manifestation of his divine existence. In order to give us an abundant life, he came into our world. Our Christian life comes from Jesus, is lived in him, and is moving constantly toward him, our goal.

We live by faith in the love of Jesus for us. In baptism Jesus united our life to his, so that we form one living being with him. In him alone, after all, is true life; there is no other redeemer to be awaited and no other way of salvation.

To reject Jesus, then, as builders reject a stone that does not please them, is to reject the very foundation of our being. We would be attempting to build apart from Jesus and therefore be building on sand; in storm and wind, that is, in the trials of life, our building would collapse (cf. Matthew 7:24-27). We ourselves would sink into the abyss of nothingness. At the same time, the cornerstone we had rejected would not simply lie where it had been thrown but would, Christ tells us, crush those who had rejected it. We have a terrible example of such a fate in the end which Judas met.

A favorite word today is "co-existence." This means reaching agreement with others, letting others go their way, setting up precise boundary markers on all sides. Another favorite word is "pluralism." This means that there are many paths by which men can reach their goal.

Why should there not be co-existence and pluralism with regard to Christ? Should we not let every man reach happiness in his own fashion? Many people are willing to let Christ have his way as long as that way pleases them. But they also want to live their daily lives in independence of him and not to be bound by his norms and his will. There are people who are quite willing to accept Christ as defender of the poor, the sick, and the sinner, but are not willing to accept him as Lord and lawgiver. They appeal to Jesus' own words: "Give to Caesar what is Caesar's" (Matthew 22:21), but they do not remember that Jesus nowhere says that Caesar need not give God what is God's.

If a man separates religion and life, Christianity and the rest of reality, he is not permitting Jesus to be the cornerstone. He is admittedly not simply rejecting Jesus, but neither has he the courage to build his whole life on Jesus and to order his life with a view to Jesus. He wants to keep his freedom and to reserve certain areas of his life to himself.

We cannot, however, simply live alongside Christ; we can only live in him, and he in us. There is no pluralism, no co-existence, that is, Christian existence alongside Jesus, but only an in-existence, that is, a life *in* Jesus.

Jesus is the foundation stone on which everything else rests and on which we must base our way of living. He is the Greater One, the Lord to whom all else is subject and who encompasses everything else. "There is no other name in the whole world given to men by which we are to be saved" (Acts 4:12). "In him we live and move and have our being" (Acts 17:28). "There is no salvation in anyone else" (Acts 4:12). We may not say, therefore: "Over here is Catholicism: be zealous for it; over there is your academic life: do well at it!" We must rather say: "Be orthodox in your work, because it too is from Jesus Christ and it is to be done in and for him." Without Jesus we can do nothing.

In using the symbol of a stone, we are by no means implying that rigidity and unchangeableness are special characteristics of Jesus. Jesus was indeed hard and inflexible when it came to the honor and will of his Father. But he was mild and gentle of heart to poor suffering and sinful men. He refused to quench the smoldering wick or to break the bruised reed.

Faith in the goodness and kindness of the Savior is the solid ground upon which Catholics can build with security. He is the Archimedean point from which they can move the world.

Mary built upon Jesus as foundation and cornerstone, for she based her life on faith in him. Peter the Apostle, whose very name was "rock," built upon this foundation, for he said: "Lord, to whom shall we go? You have the words of eternal life" (John 6:68). The holy Apostle Paul built upon this foundation, as he told the community at Corinth: "Thanks to the favor God showed me I laid a foundation as a wise master-builder might do, and now someone else is building upon it. Everyone, however, must be careful how he builds. No one can lay a foundation other than the one that has been laid, namely, Jesus Christ" (1 Cor. 3:10-11).

The history of the Church and of the saints is proof that those who build on Christ have a future before them, while those who reject him throw away the very foundation of their own lives. We must therefore construct our lives on Jesus through faith and hope. It is part of the mystery of evil that Jesus Christ the cornerstone was rejected by his own people, who cried out on Good Friday: "We have no king but Caesar" (John 19:15). But God is all-wise and directs everything, even sin, so that it eventually occasions good. This is marvelously demonstrated in the death of Jesus. The Jews of that day scorned the divine stone sent from heaven and rejected it as useless and unprofitable. They despised Jesus, shattered him, and determined to get rid of him. But God made him head and cornerstone. He made Jesus the center of the world and the keystone that holds everything together.

Jesus is thus not only the foundation and cornerstone that supports the whole building; he is also the keystone that holds it all together. Without Christ it would be impossible for the people of God to attain a perfect unity, whereas the more the members of God's people live in union with Jesus, the more closely also they are united to one another. As the keystone holds the vault of a building together, so Jesus holds men together, whether in the basic community which is the family, or in the spiritual community which is the parish, or in the Church as a whole, or in a religious Order. He is the bond of unity between priests and laity, between the religious Orders and the people at large. Without Jesus no community would have cohesion but would collapse like an arch from which the keystone has been removed. Therefore Pascal is justified in saying: "If Christ were to vanish, the world would be destroyed or become a hell." On the other hand, the more the world recognizes Jesus and the more he becomes its center, its keystone, and its goal, the more easily men are united in a community of peace. It is the ultimate and supreme purpose of the Lord that his disciples should remain intimately united to him in the closest possible union through his flesh and blood.

The account in the Acts of the Apostles of the first Christian community shows us how Jesus brings men together into unity and keeps them thus united. In Acts we are told: "The community of believers were of one heart and one mind" (Acts 4:32); "they devoted themselves to the apostles' instructions and the communal life, to the breaking of bread and the prayers" (Acts 2:42).

Over the tomb of St. Peter the Apostle rises a mighty dome, marked by the sign of Christ, the Cross. On the dome are the words: *Hinc una fides mundo refulget, hinc sacerdotii unitas exoritur*, that is: "From this spot a single faith casts its radiance over the world; here the priesthood has the source of its unity." The image is of the arches of a vault spreading out from the keystone.

With St. Peter and his successors as the center, the one faith sheds its radiance over the world. St. Peter and his successors are the center in which the priesthood is unified. This is possible, however, only because St. Peter and his successors are the vicars of Christ, since it is really from Christ that the faith and the priesthood derive their unity. He, whose sign rises above the dome, holds all together as the keystone holds the dome together.

By his redemptive actions Jesus healed and sanctified not only individual men but the very relationships between men. He formed his elect into his great family, gathered them around one table, and fed them with one bread.

In the celebration of the Holy Eucharist, Christ, the keystone, desires ever anew to unite his people and to maintain them in unity, for he wishes to bring the communion that exists among God's people to its perfect form in the communion of the saints. In heaven we will find our happiness, not as isolated individuals, but as the community of the blessed who are one in Christ.

THE LAMB

The image of the lamb is one of the most beautiful that the Scripture uses to awaken in us a trust and love of the Savior. It occurs countless times throughout the Bible.

Deep down in galleries beneath the earth, the miner sees the veins of gold gleaming as they run along between the layers of rock. In a similar way, the reader of the Old and New Testaments can see the image of the lamb whose blood is the ransom for sin running like a vein of gold through sacred history.

I

The unblemished lamb that Abel offered in sacrifice to God and the sacrificial lamb that was to be slain each year in memory of the Exodus from Egypt were both anticipatory images of the Lamb of God, Jesus Christ. John the Baptist directed the first disciples to Jesus with the words: "There is the Lamb of God!" (John 1:36). Later on St. Paul wrote: "Christ our Passover has been sacrificed" (1 Cor. 5:7). John the Evangelist, because of his friendship with Jesus, had a profound understanding of him as the Paschal Lamb. He acquired that knowledge especially because he stood by the Cross and experienced the events surrounding the death of Jesus.

At the first celebration of the Passover meal and at its repetition by later generations, thoughtful men must have asked themselves: "Why this strange prescription? Why should the Passover lamb lose its value if any of its bones are broken [Exod. 12:46]?" The prescription could not be merely a bit of whimsy on the part of the incomprehensible God of the covenant, but was to be understood as sign of, and pointer to, a coming event. As John stood beside the Cross he found the solution to the riddle. He was deeply moved when he saw the soldiers come and break the legs of the two thieves, as was customary, but pass Jesus by without breaking his legs. In this action John saw a proof that Jesus was the true Passover Lamb and the one who brought the ancient prophecy to its fulfillment. Therefore he later wrote: "These events took place for the fulfillment of Scripture: 'Break none of his bones'" (John 19:36).

Thus it is with special affection that John the Evangelist speaks in the Apocalypse of the Son of God as a Lamb. He sees the Lamb moving through heaven and hears the heavenly choir singing his praise. And of the heavenly city he writes: "Its lamp was the Lamb" (Rev. 21:23).

Jesus himself regards the image of the lamb as expressing the depths of his being and his real mission. That image was always before the eye of his mind, for he knew that he was the reality to which the image pointed: he was the true Paschal Lamb.

The mystery of Passover already overshadows the scene of the first cleansing of the Temple. The Jews demanded that Jesus justify his action, but he simply refers to the slaying of the Passover lamb at the last Passover of his life — the Lamb which he himself would be. During his public ministry Jesus was constantly referring to the sacrifice he would offer in his death. We need recall only the conversation with Nicodemus, the predictions of the Passion, and the parable of murderous vineyard tenants (Matthew 21:33-46).

"Now when Jesus had finished all these discourses, he declared to his disciples, 'You know that in two days' time it will be Passover, and that the Son of Man is to be handed over to be crucified'" (Matthew 26:1-2). Jesus knew what lay ahead for him. He could indeed have escaped the powerful hands of the supreme council, but he chose not to do so. Instead, firmly determined to fulfill the prophecy contained in the image of the Passover lamb, he went up to Jerusalem for Passover and his final celebration of that feast. The supreme council had decided only that Jesus should not be executed on the feast day lest this occasion a riot among the people (Matthew 26:5). God, however, decided that Jesus should die on the Cross on the preparation day for the feast and at about the time the lambs were being slaughtered for Passover.

The eve of his suffering and death arrived and Jesus sat down for the evening meal with his apostles. As they began the meal, he said to them: "I have greatly desired to eat this Passover with you before I suffer" (Luke 22:15). He longed for this Passover celebration with the same yearning he had for the accomplishment of his baptism of suffering. Now the hour for the Passover meal had arrived, and the Passover lamb had been offered and prepared for the Passover meal. Whole and undivided, without a single bone of it broken, the lamb had been roasted over the fire.

As Jesus looked at the Passover lamb lying before him on the platter, we may be sure he was thinking of himself as the true Passover Lamb that must be sacrificed in order to win for believers redemption from the slavery of sin and a new life of freedom. In celebrating this meal which Jesus bade his apostles and their successors do in memory of his death and resurrection (Guardini calls the meal "the everlasting presence of his death for mankind"), they would be continuing in its fulfilled form the Old Testament Passover meal.

The Church took over into her liturgy this image of the Lamb as best expressing the person of the Redeemer. Daily she invites us to the table of the Lamb, and she never celebrates the holy sacrifice of the Mass without lifting her hands in prayer to the Lamb of God. She never distributes the Holy Eucharist to the faithful without ex-

horting them: "This is the Lamb of God!" She never ter-
minates her litanies without the threefold invocation of
the Lamb of God. During the Easter season the Church
venerates the risen Lord especially under the image of the
Lamb. In all her actions she seeks the glorification of the
Lamb, and of the dying faithful she says that they are
heeding the call to the Supper of the Lamb.

The early Church saw Jesus' death as the fulfillment of the ancient Passover. Thus, Melito of Sardis (d.
180) said in an Easter sermon: "He was born as Son, led
forth as a lamb, slain as a sheep, and buried as a man; he rose
from the dead as God, uniting in himself both God and
man."

Church art depicts the Lamb over altars and on the
domes of churches, for example, in the ancient mosaics
in the Churches of St. Pudentiana, SS. Cosmas and Damian,
and St. Praxedes, all at Rome, on Hubert van Eyck's altar
in the Church of St. Bavo at Ghent, in the baroque church
at Weingarten, etc. A lamb feeding in the midst of goats and
rams reminded St. Francis of Assisi of Jesus among his
enemies; lambs hanging with tied feet from the shoulders
of men on their way to the slaughterhouse reminded him
of Jesus hanging on the Cross, and he once gave a lamb,
probably rescued from a slaughterhouse, to "Brother Ja-
coba," as he jokingly named the noble Roman widow who,
with St. Clare, followed him so closely on the path of the
imitation of Christ. Perhaps he wanted this woman to be
reminded of Jesus, the Lamb of God, and to draw from
the thought encouragement to live like a lamb. Calderón
paid homage to the Lamb of God in two of his Sacramental
Plays.

The lamb is an image of the Savior in two respects, and
to these we shall now turn.

II

The lamb expresses the helplessness, self-giving, and obedience of the Savior. What creature, after all, is weaker than the lamb, which cannot defend itself? What creature is more selfless than the lamb, which gives its wool to clothe us? It surrenders its wool for our warmth and utters no cry of protest. And what creature is more obedient than the lamb, which quietly lets itself be led to slaughter without a cry, simply in order to provide us with food?

With the enlightened vision of a prophet, Isaias wrote of the coming Redeemer: "Like a lamb led to the slaughter or a sheep before the shearers, he was silent and opened not his mouth" (Is. 53:7). A happy dispensation of God caused this passage in Isaias to be preserved among the Qumran writings and thus afforded us new evidence of its authenticity. In the Acts of the Apostles we read how the treasurer of the Ethiopian queen was reading this passage but could not understand it until Philip the deacon explained that it was a prophecy fulfilled in the crucifixion of Jesus (Acts 8:27-35).

On his Isenheim altar Matthias Gruenewald depicts the crucifixion of Jesus in all its fearfulness. At the foot of the Cross he has a slain lamb, thus indicating that Jesus is the true Lamb who sheds his blood for us on the Cross. Jesus is the price paid for our salvation.

Jesus, the Lamb, takes us into his Father's heart, for this Lamb reveals that heart to us, that infinitely good and kindly heart which is the source both of his will to forgive us and of the "folly" of sacrificing his own Son.

This Lamb, moreover, reveals to us the innermost mystery of the Son himself. Jesus accepted his suffering out of obedience to the Father's will, for, as his prayer in the Garden of Olives shows, his desire was to please the Father: "Let it be as you would have it, not as I" (Mark

14:36). Pilate condemned him to death, but he spoke not a word. The soldiers flogged him and crowned him with thorns, but he spoke not a word. They stripped him of his garments and nailed him to the Cross, but he spoke not a word. The few words he did speak during these hours were words of love and of prayer. Speaking of the death of Jesus, the Passover Lamb, St. Paul says very aptly: "Though he was in the form of God, he did not deem equality with God something to be grasped at. Rather, he emptied himself and took the form of a slave, being born in the likeness of men. . . . He humbled himself, obediently accepting even death, death on a cross!" (Phil. 2:6-8). Thus Jesus was the helpless, selfless, obedient Lamb.

The image of the lamb no longer appeals to many of our contemporaries. They see the image of the little helpless lamb as directing people to a false and sentimental piety, and they prefer images of power, such as the wolf or the eagle.

And yet anyone who understands the symbolic language of the lamb will love this image. To such a person the lamb expresses the same nobility of soul as the Cross itself, for it indicates that Jesus Christ accepted his sacrificial death, not because of helplessness and weakness, but in order to give himself most completely and to obey his Father freely and out of expiatory love.

Many people think that they must rescue the world by their own deeds and in accordance with their own will and plans. They are the prisoners of a despairing belief in the redemptive efficacy of their own actions; therefore they prefer their wisdom and will and actions to the wisdom and will and actions of God. To these people the image of the lamb says: "No, the most important thing a human being can do is to give himself selflessly in union with Jesus, to submit obediently to God, and to die with Jesus, the Passover Lamb.

The Second Vatican Council asks the people of God to follow Christ in his humiliation and, under the guidance of Christ's Spirit, to travel the way Christ has traveled before us: the way of poverty, obedience, and self-sacrifice even to the point of death. The future of the Church depends on our returning to the poor, obedient, crucified Christ. Jesus, after all, gave his life not only out of obedience to his Father but also for our sake and in our place.

Let us, therefore, take Jesus, the Paschal Lamb, as our model. In the night of the first Passover a dead person lay in every Egyptian house, while in the houses of the Hebrews there lay a dead lamb. That lamb died in place of the first-born of each Jewish household, and it was symbolic of Jesus who was to come. Because God spared the first-born of the Hebrews, every first-born Hebrew male belonged to God and had to be presented as a sacrificial offering in the Temple. There the first-born was ransomed by payment of a *lamb* or, if the parents were poor, by payment of two turtledoves. The latter choice was especially meaningful at the presentation of Jesus, since not only were the parents too poor to sacrifice a lamb, but Jesus was himself the Lamb of God and destined to be a sacrifice of expiation for all men. In our place he accepted death, as he made clear when he said: "There is no greater love than this: to lay down one's life for one's friends" (John 15:13), and when he instituted the Blessed Sacrament of the Altar: "This is my body to be given for you" (Luke 22:19), "This is my blood . . . to be poured out in behalf of many for the forgiveness of sins" (Matthew 26:28).

By his obedience Jesus atoned for our disobedience and accepted the punishment of death that should have been ours. The power of him who made all things created us; the weakness of him who became man and died on the Cross saved his creature from being lost. We can never thank him enough for this gift. By his obedience in our name and in our place Jesus has given us a splendid model of vicarious expiation.

Today we are witnessing an apostasy from God that is incalculable in its extent and effects. In this situation the little flock of God's people must see itself as called to offer adoration, praise, fidelity, and expiation in the name and place of all who are refusing these basic duties. God's people will do so by loving all the more ardently, praying all the more intensely, and striving to accomplish all the more for God, not because in pharisaic fashion they regard themselves as superior, but simply out of compassionate love. For the sake of the small company of faithful followers God will again check and moderate his punishments. Our expiation is admittedly without intrinsic value in God's sight, but when we unite it to that of Jesus, the Lamb of God, it is acceptable to the Father.

As Father Maximilian Kolbe took the place of a father of a family and went off to die in a starvation cell, so have many saints in union with Jesus accepted a life of penance until death in the name of their brothers and sisters. In this way they have allowed Jesus to continue, in and through them, his healing, expiatory, sanctifying life and death.

The first person to unite herself with the Savior in his redemptive expiation was Mary; she has been followed by a countless host of saints. The whole people of God is called upon to join them, to dedicate themselves to God in behalf of their fellow-men, and thus to follow the Lamb. This is especially true of priests and religious and of all who receive a special mission from God. In his encyclical on the Mystical Body, Pope Pius XII wrote: "This is a deep mystery, and an inexhaustible subject of meditation, that the salvation of many depends on the prayers and voluntary penance which the members of the Mystical Body of Jesus Christ offer for this intention."

What the Pope is saying is that the eternal destiny
of so many men depends upon us. Truly an awesome responsibility! It should lead to but one resolution: I will
live as a lamb, that is, I will unite my life to the Lord's
in expiatory love in order to help in the healing and sanc-
tification of men.

III

The lamb as a symbol of the Lord in the lowliness
of his earthly life is our model. The lamb as symbol of the
risen and exalted Lord is our hope, for it is a symbol of
his power, which is the power of the powerless.

Jesus underwent death and thereby conquered it.
By his suffering and dying he merited to become Lord of
the universe. "He humbled himself. . . . Because of this,
God highly exalted him and bestowed on him the name
above every other name, so that at Jesus' name every knee
must bend in the heavens, on the earth, and under the
earth, and every tongue proclaim to the glory of God
the Father: JESUS CHRIST IS LORD!" (Phil. 2:8-11).

On Patmos, John saw the risen Lord in the image
of a lamb. This Lamb was worthy to "break the seals" and
to reveal and carry out God's plan. John wrote: "Then,
between the throne with the four living creatures and
the elders, I saw a Lamb standing, a Lamb that had been
slain. . . . When he had taken the scroll, the four living
creatures and the twenty-four elders fell down before the
Lamb. . . . This is the new hymn they sang: 'Worthy are
you to receive the scroll and break open its seals, for you
were slain. With your blood you purchased for God men
of every race and tongue, of every people and nation'"
(Rev. 5:6-9).

From harsh experience Jesus knew the world and the
questions it forces upon men. But he also won a victory
of immense importance, a victory which meant that all

things to come would be under his powerful guidance. In other words, God the Father put into the hands of Jesus Christ the Conqueror the responsibility for carrying out his entire will and plan. Jesus is the great Counsellor by his word and by the example of his life. In him are all the treasures of wisdom, and his deepest wisdom is "the wisdom of the cross" (Edith Stein).

To the extent that the believer enters into Christ, the seals are broken for him too, and he comes to know the hidden meaning of events. Whoever believes in God's love that was revealed to us in Christ, and responds to that love with a dedicated heart, possesses the key to many mysteries affecting not only the world at large but his own little life in particular. Jesus does not break the seals of our life all at once but only gradually, one after another. He will break the last one only at the moment of our death, but how we will be amazed and bow down in worship of God when that final seal is broken!

Through prayer and meditation we come to understand God's plan; there, too, we can learn his will for us. To this end we must live our life, do our work, and accept our difficulties in union with Jesus and his Spirit and in accordance with his will. We must put our efforts and intentions in his hands and dedicate them to him with the words: "Jesus, I love you."

According to the Apocalypse of St. John, the Lamb also has the power to redeem men. John writes: "After this I saw before me a huge crowd which no one could count from every nation and race, people and tongue. They stood before the throne and the Lamb, dressed in long white robes and holding palm branches in their hands. They cried out in a loud voice, 'Salvation is from our God, who is seated on the throne, and from the Lamb'. . . . Then one of the elders asked me, 'Who are these people all dressed in white? And where have they come from?' I said to him, 'Sir, you should know better than I.' He then told me, 'These are the ones who have survived the great period of trial; they have washed their robes and made them white in the blood of the Lamb. . . . The Lamb on the throne will shepherd them. He will lead them to springs of life-giving water'" (Rev. 7:9-17).

The paschal lamb, prefigurative symbol of Christ the Lamb, already possesses the purifying power here described. The houses of the Hebrews in Egypt were no less filled with the poor sinful children of Adam than were the houses of the Egyptians, yet the destroying angel passed the Hebrew houses by. God spared the Israelites, not because of the blood of a holy man like Abel, Abraham, Isaac, or Jacob, nor because of the blood of a lion, the king of the animal world, but because of the blood of a lamb.

While the Hebrews, strangers without a homeland, were hastily eating the flesh of the Passover lamb, the blood of the lamb, smeared on the doorposts outside, caused them to be left in peace. That blood was a sign that warded off the anger of God as it raged through Egypt. It also overcame the anger of Pharaoh, for before the night was over he summoned Moses and told him: "Leave my people at once, you and the Israelites with you!" (Exod. 12:31). "The Egyptians likewise urged the people on, to hasten their departure from the land" (Exod. 12:33).

The blood of the Passover lamb on the doorposts points ahead to the blood of Jesus that flowed down the timbers of the Cross. The blood of Christ was already demonstrating its power under the veil of the sign that prefigured it.

Jesus is the Lamb whose blood *extinguishes the anger of God*. It purifies men of their sins. In it, as in a flowing spring, the saints wash their pilgrim robes brilliantly clean from the dust of the earth.

Jesus is the Lamb whose blood *ransomed lost man-*

kind from slavery. All men begin as slaves of sin, Satan, and death, but the Lamb sets them free. For Jesus himself became a slave in order to redeem the other slaves, and he made of the redeemed "a royal nation of priests in the service of his God and Father" (Rev. 1:6). He led them forth from the sphere of the merely human into "the glorious freedom of the children of God" (Rom. 8:21) and made of them God's holy people. Jesus is thus the source of freedom. "Where the Spirit of the Lord is, there is freedom" (2 Cor. 3:17).

Jesus is the Lamb whose blood *opens the way to heaven*. Any saint in heaven is there because he has washed his garments in the blood of the Lamb; not a single one of them has passed through the narrow gate without being marked with the radiant sign of the Lord's blood.

It was as pilgrims, with loins girt and staff in hand, that the Israelites stood around the simple table of the Passover lamb. They were making ready for the journey; indeed they were already on their way. We, too, are all on a journey. Our goal is eternity, and we are advancing toward it. Blessed are we if the blood of the Lamb shows us the way. That is why we constantly seek to cleanse our pilgrims' robes in the sacrament of penance; that is why we constantly seek strength of soul by drinking the blood of the new covenant in the Holy Eucharist.

Abel gave expression to his worship of God by sacrificing the lambs of his flock. In the Holy Sacrifice of the Mass we unite ourselves to the glorified Lamb who stands before God's throne as the Lamb that was slain. With him we offer to God the almighty Father, in the unity of the Holy Spirit, all honor and glory.

The Lamb "slain but now alive" on the heavenly altar stands before God as our mighty *intercessor*. In the Book of Job we see the accuser (that is what the word "devil" means) constantly informing against us and revealing all the evil actions of our life. But there is Another who never tires of speaking a weighty word in our behalf.

Awareness of our sins can, with good reason, make us uneasy when we think of the holy God. To him, after all, all things are plain as day. Moreover, we will receive from him what our deeds deserve. Everything hidden will be revealed. But we also know that Christ intercedes for us before the throne of God, and this knowledge relieves us of the feeling of hopelessness. We are not simply accused men and women standing before their judge; we are also friends of One who shed his blood for us, we are the people for whom Christ died. How can we despair when we have so powerful an intercessor with the Father?

The power of the Lamb *draws men to him* and makes them his followers. Surely that is the most beautiful manifestation of his power! Jesus, the Lamb of God, does not win men's souls, however, by promising them a comfortable, successful life. He wins them because he tells his chosen ones that they will have to suffer for his name's sake. Those whom he calls are filled with love of him, and therefore they follow him, heedless of the sacrifices entailed. On one occasion John the Baptist pointed Jesus out to his own disciples with the words: "Look! There is the Lamb of God!" (John 1:36), and two of these disciples immediately set out after Jesus, for while the Lord was on earth, an irresistible power went out from him. That power was to be even greater once he had been raised from the dead and exalted at the Father's side. Did he not say of himself: "And I — once I am lifted up from the earth — will draw all men to myself" (John 12:32)? In the course of history the risen Lord has drawn countless men to himself. He has done it through the power inherent in his love, for this love causes the souls he has chosen to devote themselves to him and to abandon all other loves for the sake of his.

The first to follow the Lamb was Mary. In her wake came the apostles, the martyrs, the confessors, the countless priests and religious. Someone has estimated that down to the present time there have been approximately eight million religious in the history of the Church, and we can be assured that the Lamb will in the future be mighty enough to win men for the priesthood and religious life and to keep them faithful to their calling. Who could be more powerful than the One who revealed himself through the symbol of the lamb? One religious said of his vocation: "I was especially struck by a passage from the Apocalypse that will ring in my ears as long as I live: 'They are pure and follow the Lamb wherever he goes,' singing a 'hymn no one [else] could learn.' I wanted to be with them and to sing that hymn. That was my main determination."

Happy they who accept the Lamb's invitation and surrender to his power! John was allowed to see them in their eternal joy. He wrote: "Then the Lamb appeared in my vision. He was standing on Mount Sion, and with him were the hundred and forty-four thousand who had his name and the name of his Father written on their foreheads. . . . They were singing a new hymn before the throne. . . . This hymn no one could learn except the hundred and forty-four thousand who had been ransomed from the world. These are men who have never been defiled by immorality with women. They are pure and follow the Lamb wherever he goes. They have been ransomed as the first fruit of mankind for God and the Lamb" (Rev. 14:1-4).

Let us, then, join our voices to those of the countless chosen ones from every people, tribe, language, and nation who stand singing before the throne and the Lamb. Let us unite our voices with theirs in their hymn of praise.

Hail to our God who sits upon the throne and to the Lamb!

Lamb of God, grant us to travel with you the road of obedience and reparation!

Lamb of God, break the seals of our life, intercede for us with God our Father, and offer him in our name the sacrifice of adoration! Cleanse us of all sin, and by the power of your love bring many souls to follow you!

THE JUDGE

It is a solemn moment when a judge passes sentence on a human being; the more important the judgment is for the man's future, the more solemn it is. Yet the sentence of a human judge can never be wholly perfect, because many motivations and even many circumstances of men's deeds escape the knowledge of others, while no man can pass judgment on what goes on within the minds and souls of their fellows. In addition, a human sentence is valid only for a time. Death nullifies it.

There is, however, a judge superior to any human judge, and he is Jesus. God the Father has put judgment into his hands, so that he is the judge even of judges, and his judgment is infallible. It is valid for eternity as well as time. Heaven and earth will pass away but his word will never pass away (cf. Matthew 24:35).

On the Last Day he will pass judgment on us all. We will not be able to appeal to any higher court against that judgment. But though Jesus foretold that he would come on the Last Day as judge (cf. Matthew 24:15-51), the prediction should not strike us simply as a threat; it should also be a good news, a message of life.

"An hour is coming, has indeed come, when the dead shall hear the voice of the Son of God" (John 5:25). Just when this hour will strike and the Last Day dawn, no one knows, not even the angels. Indeed, according to Mark 13:32, not even the Son knows it (because the Father has willed that the time of judgment should not be part of revelation), but only the Father (Matthew 24:36).

The Last Day will come suddenly, flashing upon us like lightning in the night. It will come unexpectedly, as the flood came in the days of Noah. Those in the fields will not return to their homes, those on the rooftops will not re-enter their houses.

"He will dispatch his angels 'with a mighty trumpet blast, and they will assemble his chosen from the four winds, from one end of the heavens to the other'" (Matthew 24:31). The marvelous trumpet blast will pierce the graves all over the earth and will summon all before the throne. Both Death and Life will stand in awe as mankind gives its answer from the grave. All the dead will rise; no one will sleep through the trumpeted summons. Almighty God, who formed man's body from the earth and breathed into it an immortal soul, has power to reunite body with soul and to breathe a new life into that body. He will raise all the dead; no one can remain deaf to his reveille.

The dead will rise up, from Abel down to the last man on the next to the last day: the dead in the cemeteries of city and village, the dead in the desert and the sea, those who died on the battlefields and in cataclysms of nature, those who died in street and shop, the young and the old, emperor and beggar.

They will be as countless as the stars in heaven or the sand on the seashore, forming one great mass of fear-stricken souls that wait breathlessly for what is to come. "Then the sign of the Son of Man will appear in the sky" (Matthew 24:30). This sign may be the Cross, for on it the Lord died for our salvation, thus making it his special sign. But the sign in the heavens may also be his heart, which symbolizes his love for us. It was to this heart that the Father wished to call our attention when he had the soldier pierce it with a lance. On that heart men's eyes will be fixed at the final Judgment. Then he himself will come; all the other events of the Last Day will be but heralds of him.

The final day which will put an end to the series

of days begun at creation, and the final day on which the last act in the drama of history will be played out, will be a great day for Jesus. Men will see him then in all his nobility and greatness, surrounded by the angels and their pealing trumpets, radiant in the light of God's glory, and coming in great power and splendor. He will be revealed in his full divine majesty. How different he will then be from the Jesus the Gospels usually show us! He will not appear as the meek, mild, and merciful Jesus, not as the divine friend of children, not as the Redeemer of sick and wounded souls, not as the Good Shepherd. Men will not see in him the Jesus who once scattered his charming parables like gleaming pearls before the crowds on the flower-clad hills around Capernaum or from his boat as it tossed on the rippling Sea of Gennesaret.

Then the appropriate words will not be those of Pilate: "Look at the man!" (John 19:5). Then, rather, we will exclaim: "Look at this God!" The crown Jesus will be wearing will not be the crown of thorns but the crown of divinity. His face will not be marred by blood and spittle, but radiant and transfigured with divine glory. In himself he contains all the beauty of heaven and earth, and the elect will gaze at him blissfully, as did the three apostles at the Transfiguration.

Instead of a purple cloak he will wear the cloak of royal power. His throne will not be a block of stone but all creation. He will be accompanied by cherubim and seraphim singing his praises, and his prophecy to Caiaphas will be marvelously fulfilled: "Soon you will see the Son of Man seated at the right hand of the Power and coming on the clouds of heaven" (Matthew 26:64).

On the Last Day all men without exception will be participants, not spectators. For the *good* it will be a day of happiness as they rise from the grave with glorified bodies. The beauty of Jesus himself will radiate from them as from a crystal (the theologians call this share in divine beauty sanctifying grace), and their good works will be revealed to all and shine like gleaming pearls. They are those who have cleansed their souls of sin in the sacrament of penance. Therefore they will be filled with joy as they raise their eyes to Jesus, for they will know that the completion of their redemption is at hand (cf. Luke 21:28).

For the *wicked* the Last Day will be a bitter day indeed, for they will be forced to see themselves as they are: deprived of sanctifying grace and deserving of God's wrath. In the light of the Last Day all that is hidden will become known: "Nothing is concealed that will not be revealed, and nothing hidden that will not become known" (Matthew 10:26). Filled with terror, the wicked will moan: "'Happy are the sterile, the wombs that never bore and the breasts that never nursed.' Then they will begin saying to the mountains, 'Fall on us,' and to the hills, 'Cover us'" (Luke 23:29-30).

For *all* men the Lord's coming will be like that of the sun when the human eye beheld it for the first time. He will say to them: "Come closer! I am Jesus, your judge! To me the Father has given power to pass judgment" (cf. John 5:27). Every human being will stand as an accused criminal before the transfigured and exalted Son of Man. So will it be, even if the individual be as perfect as St. Paul, who could say of himself: "I have nothing on my conscience. But that does not mean I am declaring myself innocent. The Lord is the one to judge me" (1 Cor. 4:4).

The grain and the weeds will have grown side by side long enough. Now the time of harvest is at hand, when it will become clear what is grain and what weed, or who have lived good lives and who evil lives. Whitened sepulchers will fool no one at the resurrection. The hour will be at hand when of two women grinding meal or two men working in the fields, one will be taken and one left. The names written in the Book of Life will be revealed, and those who thought their good works were written in the sand will see them indelibly recorded. Not a mouthful of water given to a thirsty fellow-man for Jesus' sake will be forgotten. All deeds will be weighed in the scales of justice, but only those will be heavy enough to register which have sprung from grace and the love of God. Those who have done good will receive an abundant reward; those who have gathered treasures which neither moth nor worm nor thief can destroy will rejoice in them as an everlasting possession.

The judgment will be a saving judgment. The justice that Jesus is commissioned by the Father to exercise is God's fidelity to his generous promises. Just as Jesus came the first time not to condemn but to rescue, so he will come the second time to complete our redemption.

With good reason, then, does St. Francis de Sales say: "I would rather be judged by the Savior than by my own mother."

"Then he will separate them into two groups, as a shepherd separates sheep from goats. The sheep he will place on his right hand, the goats on his left" (Matthew 25:32-33). The good, drawn by the power of his love, will advance to his right side, but a terrible pressure will drive the evil to his left. Everyone will know where he belongs. No evil person will dare try to go to Christ's right side, and none of the elect need fear being driven to the left.

"The king will say to those on his right: 'Come. You have my Father's blessing! Inherit the kingdom prepared for you from the creation of the world. For I was hungry and you gave me food. . . .'" (Matthew 25:34-35).

With inexpressible joy will the elect hear the judgment passed on them, for it will open for them the door to the everlasting wedding feast. Because they had the Father's blessing, they had been able to travel the road that truly leads to the Father. And because they endeavored to travel this road, they kept on receiving the Father's blessing. Now, in his kingdom, they will continue to enjoy his blessing and will live in the fullest possible union with him.

They will be astonished, however, and will ask the Judge how they had merited this kind of eternity. After all, they had been but unprofitable servants who had only done their duty. But the Lord will tell them the secret by declaring: "It was me you served in your suffering fellow men; it was for my sake that you served them; therefore I will serve you at the wedding banquet of heaven."

Thus heaven is indeed something earned, and anyone who has not served the Lord will be excluded from it. Heaven is a reward for cooperating with God's grace and doing the works of love.

But heaven is also a gift which God has prepared since the creation of the world. Even if we had served God for a lifetime in the most perfect way possible, we could not have merited the infinite happiness of heaven. Those who stand among the elect will recognize heaven to be a gift and will sing jubilantly: "The favors of the Lord I will sing forever" (Ps. 89-2).

Some men, however, will be condemned, as the Gospel makes clear: "Then he will say to those on his left: 'Out of my sight, you condemned, into that everlasting fire prepared for the devil and his angels!'" (Matthew 25:41). All those who spent their earthly lives on the left side, that is, traveled the paths of evil, will have to go over to the left side of the Judge. No one can stand at Christ's right side on the day of judgment if he has not walked at Christ's right side during this life. The decisive thing will be that the damned did not serve Jesus in the poor, the unhappy, the persecuted, the sick, and so on.

If love was not part of their lives, if they were people

who scorned and rejected love, then they certainly broke the other commandments as well. The result was that they were far from Christ and his commandments.

The thought of the judgment to come should shake us from our lethargy and be a stimulus to us. Contemporary man would like to be sure of a favorable judgment, and this at the least cost to himself. He would like to have that kind of judgment passed on his life without having to accede to the serious demands of the Gospel and without conversion and repentance.

But in fact it is not enough simply to have an abstract knowledge of the Gospel and of the life of Jesus Christ. One must also commit oneself to Christ and the Gospel. At the judgment some will say to Christ: "We ate and drank in your company. You taught in our streets." His answer will be: "I tell you, I do not know where you come from. Away from me, you evildoers!" (Luke 13: 26-27).

From prison at Rome, St. Paul wrote to his favorite community, the Philippians, and urged them to be joyful because the Lord was near at hand. But he also warned them to strive earnestly: "Work with anxious concern to achieve your salvation" (Phil. 2:12).

St. Jerome used to say: "I always hear the trumpets of judgment ringing in my ears!" That is, I am always thinking of the judgment to come. Whenever St. Thomas Aquinas bowed down before the Blessed Sacrament, he would say: "I adore you who will come to judge me." We should think often of judgment and live now as the friends of him who must someday act as our Judge. We should await the coming of the Lord with a lively love that controls all our powers and directs them to him whose coming we desire.

Over the main entrance of many Gothic churches we find representations of the Last Judgment. They tell anyone who enters: "You must all be judged. Only if you pass unscathed through judgment can you enter the halls of heaven which this church symbolizes."

Let us avoid judging others, and God will be kind to us when he comes to judge us. We should rather pass judgment on ourselves in the sacrament of penance, for by so doing we substitute a divine judgment inspired by mercy for a divine judgment inspired solely by justice. And let us often pray: "Lord Jesus, do not condemn me but unite me with the blessed!"

In early 1887, Johannes Kuhn, the great theologian of Tuebingen, was preparing for death. After receiving the last sacraments, he folded his hands and prayed a verse of the *Dies irae*, which would run thus in English:

> King of fearful majesty,
> your gift of saving grace is free:
> in loving mercy now save me.

THE JESUS PRAYER

The Jesus prayer is very popular in the Eastern Church. In this prayer a person devoutly repeats the Name of Jesus over and over, either orally or in his mind.

The name Jesus can be used by itself; it may also be accompanied by a short sentence. Thus the title of each chapter in this book could be connected with the Holy Name and turned into a prayer. For example: "Jesus, Son of Mary, have mercy on us!"; "Jesus, our teacher, have mercy on us!"; "Jesus, our physician, have mercy on us!"; "Jesus, our Good Shepherd, have mercy on us!"

It is possible to invoke the Name of Jesus in any place and at any time. We can do it on the street, at our place of work, in our home, in church, etc. Before we begin invoking the Name of Jesus, we should recollect ourselves and ask the Holy Spirit to guide us, since "no one can say: 'Jesus is Lord,' except in the Holy Spirit" (1 Cor. 12:3). The Holy Spirit is the power that gives the utterance of the Name its vitality and makes it a source of light for our souls.

As we repeat the Holy Name, we should gradually and peacefully focus our thoughts and feelings, indeed our whole being, on the person of Jesus. The thought of Jesus' Name should permeate our soul as a drop of oil spreads out through a piece of material until it has moistened every part of it. We must, as it were, put our whole selves into the Name of Jesus and let it become our mainstay.

The repetition of the Name of Jesus is comparable to the beat of a bird's wings as it rises into the air. When the bird has reached the height it desires, it begins to glide and needs to move its wings only occasionally in order to remain at that level. So, too, the soul that has absorbed the Name of Jesus and is filled with the thought of it can rest in the Lord. It need repeat the Name only from time to time and it will retain its intensity of devotion. Wherever we invoke the Name of Jesus, the promise is fulfilled: "I will come to you and bless you" (Exod. 20:24), for "there is no other name in the whole world given to men by which we are to be saved" (Acts 4:12). The invocation of the Name of Jesus under the influence of the Lord's Spirit will open to us the mysteries of God's love.